SLINGSHOT

MOUSTAFA HAMWI

SLINGSHOT

The Practical Guide to
Becoming a Master of Your Destiny,
Not a Victim of Your History

MOUSTAFA HAMWI

Slingshot
Copyright © 2023 Moustafa Hamwi
First published in 2023

Print: 978-1-76124-111-6
E-book: 978-1-76124-113-0
Hardback: 978-1-76124-112-3
Audiobook: 978-1-76124-114-7

All rights reserved. No part of this book may be reproduced, stored in a retrieval system, or transmitted by any means (electronic, mechanical, photocopying, recording, or otherwise) without written permission from the author.

Because of the dynamic nature of the Internet, any web addresses or links contained in this book may have changed since publication and may no longer be valid. The information in this book is based on the author's experiences and opinions. The views expressed in this book are solely those of the author and do not necessarily reflect the views of the publisher; the publisher hereby disclaims any responsibility for them.

The author of this book does not dispense any form of medical, legal, financial, or technical advice either directly or indirectly. The intent of the author is solely to provide information of a general nature to help you in your quest for personal development and growth. In the event you use any of the information in this book, the author and the publisher assume no responsibility for your actions. If any form of expert assistance is required, the services of a competent professional should be sought.

Publishing information
Publishing and design facilitated by Passionpreneur Publishing
A division of Passionpreneur Organization Pty Ltd
ABN: 48640637529

Melbourne, VIC | Australia
www.passionpreneurpublishing.com

WHAT GLOBAL LEADERS ARE SAYING ABOUT MOUSTAFA

"Moustafa is one of the great 100 Leaders and Coaches of the future."
Dr Marshall Goldsmith
World's #1 Executive Coach

"Moustafa...Mr. Passion!"
The late Prof. Tony Buzan
Inventor of Mind Mapping, Nobel Peace Prize Nominee

"It's exciting to see what you are doing Moustafa and the influence you are having on the world."
Stephen M. R. Covey
New York Times and #1 Wall Street Journal bestselling author

"One of the few individuals that truly understands the power of passion and is making a real difference in the world."
John Mattone
World's #1 Authority on Intelligent Leadership

"If I can give you one piece of advice: If you lack passion, call Moustafa!"
Fons Trompenaars
World's Leading Authority on Corporate Culture

To the soul of my late father,
Professor Hassan Hamwi:
the underdog who had a mind of
steel and an unstoppable spirit.

Your impact still lives on.

TABLE OF CONTENTS

Acknowledgments..XI
Foreword by Marisa Peer..XV
Intro – You are the Master of Your Destiny..............................1

Chapter 1
SPINNING MY WHEELS
No matter how hard I try, I take one step forward
and two steps back..7

Chapter 2
WHAT'S YOUR STORY?
Change your story, change your life..19

A. HEAL YOUR PAST

Chapter 3
WHY AND HOW TO HEAL YOUR PAST
Do not drag the worst of your past into
the best of your future..31

Chapter 4
APPRECIATE YOUR PAST
Honour your struggles; they have served you!........................41

Chapter 5
UNDERSTAND WHAT IS HOLDING YOU BACK
You have nothing to prove to anyone but yourself..................51

Chapter 6
RELEASE YOUR NEGATIVE EMOTIONAL BAGGAGE
There are no mistakes in life, only lessons learned..................61

Chapter 7
LEARN FROM THE PAST TO SLINGSHOT INTO THE FUTURE
Turn your lessons into wisdom 85

B. MASTER YOUR MINDSET

Chapter 8
WHY AND HOW TO MASTER YOUR MINDSET
What sets a mediocre person apart from those
who are extremely successful? 97

Chapter 9
BELIEVE IN YOURSELF
Who else will? 103

Chapter 10
DEAL WITH PROCRASTINATION AND SELF-LIMITING BELIEFS
The Monkey Ladder 127

Chapter 11
FOCUS ON WHAT MATTERS
Where attention goes, energy flows 141

Conclusion
DID I REALLY RELEASE MY PAST AND MASTER MY MINDSET?
Keep brushing your teeth 159

WANT MORE HELP IN MASTERING YOUR DESTINY? 165
About the Author 167
Keynotes, Workshops, and Retreats 171
One-On-One Coaching for Visionary Underdogs 173
Become a Global Thought Leader 175

ACKNOWLEDGMENTS

I owe a big thank you to a lot of people who helped this book see the light. Below, I list only a few, simply because I would need a full book to acknowledge them all.

To my family:
- Firstly, I'm grateful to my mother for instilling in me that excellence is an earned pursuit, not a birthright.
- To my sisters Bushra, Arwa and Zeina, for stepping up when times got tough.
- To my niece Seema, and nephews Omar and Hamza, for sticking together.
- To my niece Reina, for her pure loving 'Gulu'.
- To my nephew Kenz, for all the exchanges of pure laughter.
- And to Yousef, for giving me a lot of reasons to ask, "Who do I want to be in these darkest of times?".

To my mentors*:
- Dr John DeMartini, who inspired me to heal my past and see the blessings in every situation. A lot of the techniques in this book were inspired by your teachings.
- Dr Marshall Goldsmith, for always reminding me that the pursuit of a higher purpose requires courage, humility, and discipline.
- The late Prof. Tony Buzan, for honouring me with the title 'Mr Passion' and for the valuable impact Mind Mapping has had on my life.

To my healers, guides and therapists:
- Anand Raj, for introducing me to Tai Chi and living the true Zen and guiding me always with a smile.
- Bela Dubbelman, for always being there for me and introducing me to Primal Deconditioning.
- Dhyan Shikha, for the best bodywork that connected me with my inner being.
- Diana Azavedo, for the smooth progress with my yoga.
- Guru Yoganda of Vashish, for the lessons from the caves and asking me questions that changed my life and set me on this journey.
- Dr Heather Warwick, for keeping my body moving.
- Ian Cariaga, for bringing out the jacked yogi in me.
- Swami Sanjeev Krishna, for my first-ever induction to proper yoga.
- Zarine Dadachanji, for the genuine care and most amazing sound healing.
- All my teachers at the Australian Yoga Academy, for believing in me and helping me bounce back to my yogi self.

To my friends*:
- Anita Anand, for your sisterly love.
- Gautam Ganglani, for the continuous support throughout my journey.
- Gökçe Gediktas, for being a great and supportive friend.
- Kylie Mata, for stepping up to help when I needed it the most.
- Lisanna Weston, for the amazing support on my executive nomad journey.
- Noirin Mosley, for being my greatest ambassador.

ACKNOWLEDGMENTS

- Rosa G. Aygun, for always believing in me.
- Sam Farhang, for your care and being a great companion.
- Saqr M. Ereiqat, for being a trusting brother and a visionary business partner.
- Sharaf Goussous, for the continuous brotherly care.

And thanks to my team* that helped me make this book as good as it can be:
- Cat Martindale-Vale, for the amazing publishing management.
- Charles Tan, for the amazing publishing support.
- Dorie Racelis, for the great market research.
- Harika Bantupalli, for the usual commitment.
- Lolita Catabui, for keeping our CRM in top shape.
- Nesty Faith, for keeping our finances in order.
- Dr Scott Hurley, for being my diligent and trusted editor.
- Shobha Nihalani, for the valuable review and feedback.
- Timothy Roberts, for the diligent proofreading.
- The whole team at Passionpreneur Publishing, who made this book see the light.

And to the whole Passionpreneur Author Tribe, I'm still on this journey because of you.

Finally, to everyone who supported me but I couldn't mention on this page, know that in my heart, I will always appreciate your support.

---

* Everyone's name, aside from my family's, is mentioned in alphabetical order.

FOREWORD BY MARISA PEER

GLOBALLY ACCLAIMED THERAPIST, BESTSELLING AUTHOR, AND AWARD-WINNING SPEAKER

In my work as a therapist, I spent over three decades treating a client list that includes international superstars, CEOs, royalty, and Olympic athletes. I love to see people awaken empowerment and unlock rapid transformation in their lives. This has led me to combine the best elements of cognitive behavioural therapy, neurolinguistic programming and hypnotherapy to create Rapid Transformational Therapy. I use RTT to help people identify, challenge, and replace their limiting beliefs and shut down their inner critic for good.

So I firmly believe in the power of the mind to create the future. But this never comes from ignoring the past or denying its existence. Rather, it comes from being able to look at the limiting beliefs this may have created in you and then replace them with empowering, transformational beliefs that can form the foundation for a more successful, happy, joyful, stronger you.

That's why I love Moustafa's work – he tackles the very important topic of dealing with your emotional baggage, and he does it in a simple and practical way.

Through this book, Moustafa helps you to step back to heal your past, and then master your mindset so you can enjoy a more fulfilling life.

Marisa Peer
Globally Acclaimed Therapist, Bestselling Author, and Award-Winning Speaker.
Founder and creator of RTT® – a new, exciting, and multi-award-winning therapy taking the world by storm.

INTRO

YOU ARE THE MASTER OF YOUR DESTINY

"Passionate people do not wait for life to happen to them; they happen to life."

—MOUSTAFA HAMWI

Fellow passionate underdog,

If you have ever felt like an underdog seeking transformation in your life, then the interactive process in this book will give you the instant results you seek, allowing you to release your past and master your mindset so you can get excited about life again. From there, you're ready to launch – and get what you truly deserve in success and recognition.

I am honoured to serve you because you are committed and dedicated to living the most passionate life possible by gaining mastery of your life instead of falling victim to your past. And I promise you I will deliver; I will make this worthwhile for you.

For those of you who do not know me yet, I'm Moustafa Hamwi, known globally for popularizing the term "Passionpreneur".

I have helped thousands of people who are seeking their purpose; I have seen them move from being lost, confused, and disoriented about the direction of their career, relationships, or lifestyle to waking up every morning and loving every aspect of their life!

Through this book, you have the opportunity to access a world-class process you can use at any stage in your life for both personal and business growth. It's one that you can repeat any time you need; think of it like going to a teeth-whitening session every now and then.

YOU ARE AWESOME!

Before we start, let me tell you that you are awesome. Put all that hesitation and self-doubt about success aside. You know why? Because you are here today trying to pursue a more passionate life and become the master of your destiny instead of a victim of your history.

You have invested money, time, and effort to read this book and do the exercises to release the past and master your mindset. In doing so, you have taken the first step. Trust me when I say that you are already ahead of the game – ahead of most people in this world. Kudos to you for that!

BUT – there's always a 'but' – this book will *not* help you unless you are serious about making a change in your life.

This book isn't for everyone. It isn't for people who want to gain health, financial breakthroughs, business advances, or relationship goals without doing the work. It isn't for people who want to ride on other people's coattails to succeed without effort. There are enough get-rich-quick schemes out there to entrap people like that. They promise the world and deliver few if any results.

This book is for people who are willing to do the work. Releasing your past, mastering your mindset, and getting to a place where you can live the life you dream of is simple. That doesn't necessarily mean easy, or effortless. The beauty of this simplicity is that anyone starting from any state of being can do it. It's just a question of whether you *will*.

HOW TO USE THIS BOOK

This book is intentionally designed to be interactive; the days of a book being nothing but a collection of theories are long gone. *SLINGSHOT* becomes more personalised based on how you interact with it. After all, your passionate life is yours and nobody else's!

To start with, a UCLA Neuroimaging Study[1] has confirmed that putting feelings into words produces therapeutic effects in the brain. And much academic research shows that activities combining

---

1   https://newsroom.ucla.edu/releases/Putting-Feelings-Into-Words-Produces-8047.

thinking and handwriting are calming to the parasympathetic nervous system; doing this is very beneficial to the self-directed neuroplasticity that rewires your brain.

You can do the exercises in this book and work at your own pace. But first, I will share my story and explain how this book came about. It provides context for the lessons that will follow, and I hope it will provide inspiration for you to hang on when things get tough. The process in this book is simple, practical, and effective.

You take a step back to release your past (this is the first part of the book) and then take two steps forward to master your mindset and own your future (the second part of this book).

This book is part of a series around designing and living the best life you can. My previous international bestselling book, *Live Passionately*, helps you design how you want to live your life on your own terms. This book, *Slingshot*, helps you release anything stopping you from living that life, in the past or the future.

To empower you further, I've curated an exclusive Empowerment Bonus Pack. This pack includes a guided meditation audio, along with a script that you can personalise; free copies of all three of my bestselling books, *Live Passionately*, *The Guided Author*, and *Slingshot*; and a comprehensive guide on breaking free and transforming your passion into a business you'll love.

Plus, I continuously update this pack with additional tools, ensuring you're equipped to live your most passionate life. Simply go to www.Moustafa.com/Slingshot or scan the QR code below and enter the code PASSION.

The fact that you are holding this book is the greatest evidence that you are ready to take full ownership of your life and transform it into the greater and grander life it is meant to be.

Scan this QR code to download your bonus pack

I AM HONOURED TO SERVE YOU

I promise you that by the time you are done with the work in this book, you are going to release many of the burdens from your history and regain mastery over your destiny. You will be a crucial part of our Passionpreneur movement – a movement of passionate entrepreneurs who are changing the world and living an amazing life while doing it.

Until then, always remember YOU ARE a master of your destiny, not a victim of your history.

Moustafa Hamwi
Bestselling Author, International Speaker, and Mindset Coach.
Hypnotherapist, Yoga and Meditation Teacher.

CHAPTER 1

SPINNING MY WHEELS

No matter how hard I try, I take one step forward and two steps back

> *"If someone is prettier than me, that's God's creation; but if they excel more than me, that's my creation."*
>
> —MAISSOUN (MY MOTHER)

Throughout my life, both professional and personal, my dreams were bigger than my means. I wanted to excel where everybody told me I would fail. I wanted to pursue passions that seemed impossible and careers where success for someone like me was improbable. After all, what is life if we cannot manifest our best hopes, dreams, and aspirations?

My mother used to say, "If someone is prettier than me that's God's creation, but if they excel more than me, that's my creation," and that made me always strive to be better against all the odds. I faced my fears head on and pushed through challenges to break any ceiling and any limitations that faced me. I loved the feeling of continuous learning and growth. If I had a weakness, I did what I had to do to get over it. I took every possible course, attended every seminar, read every book, and watched every documentary until I not only got better but also turned that weakness into strength.

Yet sometimes, no matter how hard I worked or what I tried, it felt like something was still holding me back. It was not a glass ceiling. If it was, I would have broken through it. It felt more like I was tied by a rubber band that would only allow me to run so far – a temporary feeling of growth – before snapping me back to where I started.

SPINNING MY WHEELS

With enough willpower, I would dust myself off and try again, yet too many of these rubber-band moments simply left me drained and depressed. I'm sure you know what I'm referring to. It's that promotion you kept working hard for, but always went to someone else. It's that person you have a crush on, but they have their eyes on someone else. It's those few stubborn kilos that seems not to want to leave you, or the investment strategy that seems always to fail to hit the mark.

When I was in my twenties, I had all the time and energy in the world. Add that to my constant stubbornness and determination, and it's no surprise that I would simply keep working harder and searching for new solutions. However, as I got to my late thirties this pattern started to get depressing. I started questioning myself: "Am I just doomed in some areas of my life? Are some goals just not meant to be? But this cannot be!" I was a big believer that we make our own destiny and that 'mind over matter' makes us greater than our circumstances. All the self-help gurus were teaching it, all the inspirational speakers were speaking about it, so why couldn't I make it happen?

This drove me to turn my gaze backwards. I thought: "Maybe the issue is not in my future; maybe it is some trauma I had in my past." As you can imagine, I went into the healing space with the same passion as I did everything else. I jumped from one retreat to the next, going through every conventional therapy and esoteric healing methodology I could find. I did hypnotherapy, Theta healing, energy work, Reiki, laughter meditation, crying therapy, silent meditations, journaling, water fasting, solitude in the mountains for days, and everything you might have read about, or never even heard of.

My journey through this healing world could fill a book by itself, but I just want to offer a glimpse into the depth of work that was done before writing this book. I went on this pursuit for years, travelling different parts of the world and spending tens of thousands of dollars, digging into the past trauma to see how deep the rabbit hole went.

I was determined to get to the bottom of it so I could move forward with my life and get to my goals. But it was like peeling an onion; every healing session only revealed a new layer that needed to be healed! As great as the momentary relief was from every healing work I did, I would simply see more of what was wrong with my past – and so on to the next healing work. This endless journey became just as depressing. To see more and more issues, with no end in sight, it's like looking for an exit inside a hole: the more you dig, the deeper the hole got and therefore the harder to get out of.

Well, a few years into this, and with lots of money gone, I simply realised that most of these healing methodologies overpromise total transformation – but it's not realistic. Firstly, all of it requires a lot of deep work that can extend for months or even years. And I was, in fact, prepared to spend that time, buying a one-way ticket to India to heal myself. But I realised as soon as you take a person out of the specialised healing space and put them back into their real life, they simply snap back to their old self. Context is important.

Secondly, although the deep, drastic changes over a short period of time are necessary for these therapies to work, they create identity crises. In the pursuit of comfort and certainty, people revert to the old self which leads to depression, and they think: "This works for everyone else, why is it not working for me? I must be the problem!" And they move on to the next healing workshop, down another rabbit hole to another unsatisfying Wonderland, with no end in sight.

THE PROBLEM WITH THE SELF-HELP INDUSTRY

When I started reflecting on this journey of taking one step forward and two steps back, I realised that there is an inherent bottleneck in the way the whole self-help industry is set up. There are two camps. Coaching is mainly focused on succeeding in the future through sheer willpower and determination, totally ignoring how your past can truly hold you back. The healing focuses mainly on healing your past, without acknowledging how the *present* is what creates the future.

That is when I had my *Aha!* moment. What if these solutions are not about either/or? What if it's not just about healing past trauma, nor just about focusing on a bright future? What if it's both in tandem? Life is Yin and Yang. The sea is about ebb and flow. Growth is about going through the hard times, before getting to the good. Seeds grow roots before they grow into trees.

What if I willingly chose to take *one step back* before taking *two steps forward*, instead of the opposite being forced on me? This made me realise that another, better analogy had been in plain sight the whole time – the SLINGSHOT. A slingshot requires you to pull back before you can release an object to fly great distances.

When I saw this, I started to make amazing breakthroughs, both in my personal life and in my career.

I stopped spinning my wheels in the sand, trying to achieve growth only to be wasting energy. I took the best of the lessons I learned from both worlds – about the relief you get from releasing your past trauma, about the subconscious conditioning that rules your life without you understanding why you follow repeating patterns. I went about developing a new way to do things, a realistic way, one applicable to all aspects of your current life context, be it family, work, social life, etc. It's a practical approach to changing the mindset of the past instead of drowning in a sea of memories that never end. It's simply about rewriting the stories and the point of view of the past.

Once the ground is clear and stable, the system then deploys executive coaching and mindset mastery techniques that propel us into the future. The real difference is in how this system is structured. Again, it's simple and practical. Most importantly, it is applied when you are in your real-life context, free of previous negative memories. It's like planting the same seed in more fertile ground – surely the quality of the fruit will be different.

All of this gave me a mantra developed from the teachings of my mentor Dr John Demartini, one of the world's leading human behaviour specialists. I repeat it loudly to myself, and will remind you to do the same in every chapter of this book:

"I am the master of my destiny, not a victim of my history."

The more I went through the process of healing the past and mastering my mindset, the better my quality of life became – both on the personal and the career front. I had less internal resistance and greater excitement, I procrastinated less and achieved more, I appreciated my past struggles and started noticing how they made me who I am today.

This process helped me regain my energy to spread passion around the world, accelerating my goal of becoming an international speaker, coach, and author. There were several key factors to my subsequent global success. First and foremost, the inner clarity resulting from this healing process was decisive. Without mastering my mindset, none of my other efforts would have yielded valuable results. Following the Slingshot process gave me the emotional clarity and energy needed to go from *begging* to be on stage to charging thousands of dollars for a single *hour* of my time on stage.

I created several online courses in different languages and authored many bestselling books, leading me to launch one of the world's leading publishers of transformational books – Passionpreneur Publishing, dedicated to helping other inspiring leaders share their message with the world.

SLIPPING INTO A SECOND-TIME IMPOSTER SYNDROME

Here, I'd like to share a little secret about myself. After writing the first draft of the book you're reading, I...stopped. Slipping into imposter syndrome mode, I left the whole project on the back burner. I was filled with doubts, worried that I was becoming too egotistical about the amazing benefits of the Slingshot process. Even with the success of my previous bestselling book *Live Passionately* book, I couldn't bring myself to finish this one.

A few years went by and the pandemic hit. I had just come out of a divorce and moved from Dubai to Australia to settle in Melbourne, which at that time became the world's most locked-down city. I was alone and stuck within four walls with no family, no friends, and no possibility of making new ones due to all the restrictions.

To make things worse, at the very moment I had finally reached the peak of my dream career as a speaker, the pandemic meant no more live events, which meant no speaking engagements. My publishing business was flowing smoothly, but took a sudden when the pandemic hit. Executives were losing jobs and entrepreneurs were shutting down businesses, pushing publishing way down my clientele's priority list. Just as I had finally started to taste the fruits of my labour, it was all snatched away from me.

If that wasn't enough, I faced a worse tragedy. My father caught COVID, ending up in ICU when visiting Dubai while I was in lockdown in Melbourne. Due to the travel restrictions, I was unable to get out in time to see him before he passed away. Then, just as I arrived in Melbourne after dealing with the emotional fallout, my mum was hospitalised due to a sudden series of brain strokes.

Eventually, there was only so much I could handle. The extreme pressure of these years led to a nervous breakdown.

During those challenging times, I started seeking some answers that would help me maintain my sanity. While searching for tools to help me heal and deal with everything I was going through, I had a moment of clarity. A voice in my head told me: "Practice what you preach".

In this moment of truth, I remembered the manuscript I had set aside. I pulled it out and started going through the process of healing my past and mastering my mindset. Once I got myself back on track during the pandemic, I managed to double the publishing business year on year. We went from 25 to 50 authors, then to 100+. I secured a series of virtual speaking engagements, charging thousands of dollars to deliver inspirational talks online. On the personal front, I used the lockdown period to reach the peak of my health – so much so that now, in my 40s, I am fitter and healthier than I was in my 20s.

Those challenging experiences were the triggers that helped bring this manuscript to life – my own Slingshot.

By sharing this story, I am not intending to brag about my success; I am simply telling you that the proof is in the pudding. What I have developed *works*. It worked for me, it worked for the hundreds of people I have personally coached through this system, and it worked for the thousands using it through my online courses. All have seen immediate results in their mindset and achievements.

My mission has always been about spreading passion and purpose into the world and delivering it with instant and measurable impact. I am so committed to spreading passion around the world that I have explicitly announced a BHAG – a Big, Hairy Audacious

Goal – of spreading passion to 7,777,777 people. Am I going to get to over seven million in a few years? I'm not sure how long it will take, but since I know that I have dedicated my life to this purpose, I will get there sooner or later. My philosophy is this:

> "Live life so fully that it is a life worth dying for."
>
> —MOUSTAFA HAMWI

I would love to help you on this journey of healing your past and mastering your mindset for a couple of reasons. For starters, I am fed up with the sea of self-proclaimed coaches and self-help gurus promising the sun, the moon, and the stars – yet all they do is dump lots of theory and concepts that create confusion. I've been in this system, and the whole experience left a bitter taste in my mouth. I'm sure you will have experienced some of what I am describing.

WHAT'S IN IT FOR ME?

A big personal benefit in sharing all this learning relates to the knowledge that one cannot have a party on one's own. The world needs more passionate people for this movement to become fun and to become mainstream.

> "When you reach the top, you should remember to send the elevator back down for the others."
>
> —EDITH PIAF

So, when I figured out a practical way to help slingshot me out of my trauma into the realm of mastery, I felt obliged to share my system with fellow underdogs – people who would not spare anything in the pursuit of their dreams, but who needed something that simply works!

The process in this book is simple, practical, and effective. You take a step back to release your past (this is the first section of the book) and then take two steps forward to master your mindset and own your future (which is the second part of this book).

It's a process you can use at any stage in your life, for both personal and business growth, and a process that you can repeat. Think of it like going for a teeth-whitening session every now then.

If you have ever felt like an underdog seeking transformation in your life, then the interactive process in this book will give you the instant results to release your past and master your mindset. Then you can get excited about life again and get what you truly deserve in success and recognition.

It will simply help you become the master of your destiny, not a victim of your history.

See you in the next chapter, where we will start with healing and releasing your past.

Meanwhile, to empower you further, I've curated an exclusive Empowerment Bonus Pack. This pack includes a guided meditation audio along with a script that you can personalise, free copies of all three of my bestselling books including *Live Passionately*, *The Guided Author*, and an e-copy of *Slingshot*, and a comprehensive guide on breaking free and transforming your passion into a business you'll love.

Plus, I continuously update this pack with additional tools, ensuring you're equipped to live your most passionate life. Simply go to www.Moustafa.com/Slingshot or scan the QR code below and enter the code PASSION.

Scan this QR to download your bonus pack

CHAPTER 2

WHAT'S YOUR STORY?

Change your story, change your life

> "You create your story, you live in that story, and if you don't like the story, only you can change it ... You are the only one who can change your world."
>
> —DON MIGUEL RUIZ

Understanding your story and its recurring themes, and identifying the reasons that hold you back, are just preparations for the *actual* process of healing. If you don't grasp the fundamentals, the entire process will be rendered useless.

In this chapter, we will talk about getting in touch with your story, understanding how traumatic events hold you back from having the future you want, and what you need to do to release your emotional baggage and pursue that passionate life you have always wanted. You will also be introduced to the four-step process that helps you honour your struggle, find out what is holding you back, and turn your lessons into workable wisdom.

Doing this will require a lot of energy. So, how do you make sure you have enough of it? Keep in mind that the power plant does not have energy, it *generates* energy. You can be the same!

So, are you ready to take this journey with me?

Before we start the healing process, we need to understand the story you have been telling yourself about your life.

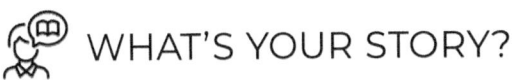 WHAT'S YOUR STORY?

Everyone has a story to tell, just like the movies we see and the novels we read. If your life was a movie, what genre would it belong to? Would you say it was a drama? A comedy? A romance? A tragedy? An adventure? Or any other genre? Go ahead and write down the genre in the worksheet. And what you would name your movie?

IF YOUR LIFE SO FAR WAS A MOVIE, WHAT GENRE WOULD IT BE?

- ☐ Drama
- ☐ Comedy
- ☐ Romance
- ☐ Tragedy
- ☐ Adventure
- ☐ Other: ....

What would you name that movie?

....

I would say that with everything I've gone through, my life is an adventure. If anything, I would call it a life to die for. Maybe at a certain point, I would have seen my life as a drama. I recall times when I would have called it *Dreams Broken on the Shores of Reality*. When this was my movie, my life was manifesting in that way. Be honest with yourself: What is your movie now? Tell me, what is your story? What is the story that you're telling yourself right now about why you're not living a fulfilling, passionate life?

Now, I want you to fill in the worksheet on the next page to help you understand your story so far.

Let me give you my version of this. My early story may have been something like this. "I am a failure in life because my family never invested in sending me to a proper university and my social setting was not very open-minded. I was not living in a space where I was learning and advancing. As for my work, I was in a very small local company that never offered me an opportunity to work in the international way I wanted. I also had responsibilities; I had to pay bills and I had to take care of things, and this was what my life was all about."

Now, it's honesty time. It's essential that you consciously know the story that you tell yourself and the world about why you're not living a passionate life. Go ahead and fill in the given worksheet on the next page.

A couple of things to note:
- The prompts i give on the sheet are to help structure your thinking about elements that impact the story you tell yourself (family, social, work, responsibilities, etc...) otherwise the story could end up more of a rant, we need a structured story to help you work on changing it in the following chapters.
- You might end up needing more space than provided on the following pages so feel free to use an external notebad if needed.

WHAT'S YOUR STORY?

 **MY STORY**

I am ....

....

....

....

Because my family ....

....

....

My social setting ....

....

....

SLINGSHOT

Work ....

....

....

....

Responsibilities (family, spouse, kids) ....

....

....

....

Other ....

....

....

....

Once you've written your story, I want you to reflect on it for a while and tell me this: What are the two or three specific themes that keep recurring in that story? Start from the top. Tell me which one recurs most, what's second, and which is the third most recurring theme in your life.

In the story I just shared, about not being properly educated and not being in the right setting, the first theme would be that people have messed up my life. There always seemed to be somebody who screwed something up in my life. The second most prominent theme would have been that my settings never supported me – my job, my career, my surroundings, my university.

You can see that these are things you need to start thinking about. I understand this is going to take a little bit of deep diving, so feel free to spend some time over this exercise. However, make sure you are doing it in *writing*. Do *not* skip through; be present with me and do the work with your hand.

Few more things to note:
- Writing your story will most probably be an emotional experience because it will stir up memories you were trying to forget, and that is ok. The true healing happens by going "through" the emotions, not "over" them.
- You will probably continue to feel vulnerable throughout the healing part of the book, be gentle and loving with yourself.

WHAT WERE THE TWO OR THREE SPECIFIC THEMES THAT KEPT RECURRING?

Rank your themes from most to least recurring

Most Recurring

Second Most

Third Most

HEAL THE PAST AND CHANGE YOUR LIFE

It is only when you acknowledge your past, embrace it, and learn from it that you can heal yourself and change your life forever. Yes, you might need some help to do this – that's what I'm here for.

Here are the steps involved in the process of healing your past, which we will discuss in detail in the coming section of the book

1. **Appreciate your past.** This is where you learn to acknowledge what happened to you in the past, embrace it, and honour all the struggles you have gone through, because they made you the strong person that you are today.

2. **Understand what has been holding you back.** Here, you delve into the aspects of the past that have been stopping you from being the person you truly want to be.

3. **Release the emotional baggage.** Learn how to let go of all the pain and anxiety and various other forms of emotional baggage that have been exhausting you for a long time now.

4. **Learn from the past and move into the future.** In this step, you will understand that there are valuable lessons in each of the struggles and traumas you have endured in life. You will learn from them and use them as a tool to move forward into the future you have always wanted.

I am here to guide you through every single step, hold your hand, and walk you through the journey of healing so you can move towards the destination of a better, happier life. In the next chapter, we will discuss the first step in detail. I will show you how to appreciate your past and honour your struggles. You will also be doing a few fun exercises to help you understand it all on a deeper level.

Are you ready to release your past? Just turn to the next chapter.

But before you do so, say it out loud:

> "I am the master of my destiny, not a victim of my history. I have courage, humility, and discipline."

A.
HEAL YOUR PAST

THE HEALING PROCESS IS FOR YOU IF:

 You feel stuck in your past.

 You want to get past the drama in your life.

 You are doing everything right, but 'something' is still holding you back.

 You want to get rid of emotional baggage that is holding you down.

 You are holding on to fears and insecurities from a past experience.

 Certain people or events trigger a strong reaction that your logical mind can't explain.

CHAPTER 3

WHY AND HOW TO HEAL YOUR PAST

Do not drag the worst of your past into the best of your future

> *"We are products of our past, but we don't have to be prisoners of it."*
>
> —RICK WARREN

Over the years, I have discovered that most people are stuck in their own stories and heartbreaks. I even include past versions of myself in that statement. Having feelings and emotions is normal, but getting stuck in such stories for way too long is *not* normal. The self-protection mechanism has a valuable function in our life. When you get a slight burn from fire, the minor trauma keeps the burn memory fresh in your mind. This helps you avoid being burned again. This is a great protection mechanism.

But such traumatic experiences can turn into dramatic memories, which slowly become addictive and start ruling your life, which is not good!

The first section of this book is about dealing with the old internal crap that is getting in the way of you living the most passionate life ever. It will also help prepare you to slingshot yourself into a future full of wonderful possibilities.

You will go through exercises to break down and decondition old patterns, and you will go through forgiveness exercises to clear you of the ties binding you to the past.

I have to tell you that this is going to take a bit of necessary hard work. You are going to dig in deep into your own shit and bring out the dirty laundry. It's going to be the best thing you can do for yourself. So be ready to go deep and do the emotional work.

This is going to require some deep leadership qualities I learned from my mentor, Dr Marshall Goldsmith:

 Courage: To look in the mirror and own up to your results.

 Humility: To ask for help when you need it.

 Discipline: To do what it takes, no excuses.

So with this, come up with your own Slingshot mantra:

> *"I am the master of my destiny, not a victim of my history. I have courage, humility, and discipline."*

Please note this is not just some cool-sounding catchphrase for social media; you will need to keep saying it throughout this book. Trust me, you will need it to achieve the level of mastery you desire.

THE PROCESS OF HEALING YOUR PAST

"If you are busy focusing on the falling bricks, you will never realize that they are truly steppingstones you need to cross over to the next phase of your life."

—KEMI SOGUNLE

The healing exercises in this section have been distilled from the best of the best of what I have learned across the globe, and I owe it to all my healers, teachers, and mentors.

The best way to simplify this healing philosophy is in the words of Dr John Demartini, one of the world's leading human behaviour specialists.

> *"Look at how your life serves you, it's on-the-way not in-the-way. You're not a victim of your history when you take the time to transform your perceptions. It's not what happens to you, it's how you perceive it. You have command over how you perceive what you've experienced. Be a master of your destiny, it's your choice."*

The process of healing your past depends on taking a step back before taking two steps forward. So the process we will go through is:

Appreciating your past and honouring your struggles; they have served you!

 Understanding what is holding you back. You have nothing to prove to anyone but yourself.

 Releasing your negative emotional baggage. There are no mistakes in life, only learning.

 Learning from your past to slingshot into the future. Turn your lessons into wisdom and rewrite your story.

LIFE IS NOT JUST POSITIVE

Life isn't an easy ride. We experience many ups and downs as we go through the years — both in our professional and personal lives. Of course, things we label as positive are usually easier to deal with. You get a promotion, find your ideal life partner, or become a parent. You are filled with joy and a desire to celebrate the happiness with your loved ones. You try and make sure that this positive phase lasts as long as possible.

However, the truth of life is that it isn't just about the positives. There will be instances where you experience events that are traumatic or extremely difficult to overcome. It might be the loss of a job, the failed attempts at a lifelong dream, or the death of a loved one. Coping with these situations is not easy, and they might send you spiralling into a web of depression you don't know how to get out of. This affects all the possibilities that the future holds.

DON'T LET YOUR TRAUMA BECOME YOUR DRAMA.

If you are still trapped in your past, you will never find a new future. If you do not consciously resolve these patterns learned in times of heartbreak or trauma, then you are bound to keep repeating them. This leads back to familiar territory time and time again, which becomes like quicksand that traps you. Think of the toxic relationships we keep getting into, or the bad credit card habits we try to get rid of.

So, before we go further, let's check if you are stuck in one of life's great potholes.

To do so let me ask you four questions that will help you understand that *maybe* you are stuck in your past trauma without even knowing:

Have your past experiences conditioned your mind and emotions to behave a certain way, and you can't get yourself out of it?

☐ Yes   ☐ Maybe   ☐ No

Do certain people or events trigger a strong reaction that your logical mind can't explain?

☐ Yes   ☐ Maybe   ☐ No

Are you holding onto fears and insecurities from a past experience?

☐ Yes   ☐ Maybe   ☐ No

Are you doing everything right, but 'something' is holding you back?

☐ Yes   ☐ Maybe   ☐ No

I am sure at least one of these questions resonated with you and sent your mind into contemplation mode. But let me tell you, trauma isn't uncommon; every human experiences it now and then in their lifetime. One thing I have discovered throughout my journey is that people get stuck in their own stories and traumas, and I am no exception to that.

Let me explain to you the emotional trauma vortex people become stuck in.

If you burn your hand in the fire, then you should remember that this is not a good experience. But when we become trapped behind a fear of multiple things and easily dragged into reliving difficult moments, our response to trauma is no longer helpful.

When we use the same trauma-forged mechanism to remember everything that happens in life, it becomes a problematic pattern. When something happens that makes you upset, you get frustrated with it. When you get frustrated with it, you get angry. When you get angry you get sad. When you get sad you get frustrated again, and the more frustrated you become, the more you become cynical.

Then it becomes a repeating self-fulfilling prophecy. You're just looping on and on in the same emotions. Finally, these emotions build a story. That story becomes the narrative that you live by, because you've been living it for so long, with so much strength, energy, and emotion, that it starts defining you.

Although it might sound counterintuitive, there is a logical reason behind all this. The psychological phenomenon known as 'Negative Bias' is our tendency not only to register negative stimuli more readily than positive ones, but also to dwell on those negativities.

It's a result of evolution. Although we have been fairly civilised as humans for a decent amount of time, prior to that we were more subject to natural dangers like wild animals. The limbic brain is hardwired to protect us by paying attention to bad, dangerous, and negative threats in the world. For most of human history, this was literally a matter of life and death. Those who were more attuned to danger and who paid more attention to the bad things around them were more likely to survive.

This meant they were also more likely to hand down those genes to their offspring which made them more attentive to danger, so they could live longer and better lives. We know that we are no longer surrounded by sabre-toothed tigers, so all we have to do is reprogram our minds if we put in the effort to do so. Yet few of us ever master this skill.

By now, I hope you have a basic understanding of how trauma works, and how such coping mechanisms can send us into an emotional vortex.

To escape it, we must consciously bring in patterns to interrupt these mechanisms and make new habits.

For now, to help instil this belief, please say it out loud:

> "I am the master of my destiny, not a victim of my history. I have courage, humility, and discipline."

CHAPTER 4

APPRECIATE YOUR PAST

Honour your struggles; they have served you!

> "Sometimes it takes a heartbreak to shake us awake and help us see we are worth so much more than we're settling for."
>
> —MANDY HALE

APPRECIATE YOUR PAST AS IT IS AND HONOUR YOUR STRUGGLES – THEY HAVE SERVED YOU!

We agree that if you want to slingshot into the future, you need to heal your past.

Healing requires genuine intention, so I am going to ask you a straight-up question and I would like you to give me a loud answer. Yes, out loud. Are you ready to release your past? Take a deep breath before answering it.

If the answer is no, please be honest and take a moment to reflect. What is it in your past that you're holding onto so tightly that you cannot release it? If you're not ready to release your past, you might want to push 'pause' on your life now. I don't mean that with regard to this book only. If you've decided to hold onto your past, with whatever drama it holds, and keep blaming circumstances and other people for whatever has happened to you, that means your whole life is pretty much on hold.

APPRECIATE YOUR PAST

Now, take as long as you want – be it five minutes, an hour, two days, a week or even a month – and stop here now. Close the book. Open it again only when you are ready to take responsibility for how you're going to move on with your life by letting bygones be bygones.

If you want to change your life, you simply have to change your story. It's that simple.

If you are ready to release your past and move on with your future, you need to start with the first step: to appreciate your past as it is and honour the struggle that has served you.

For you to do that, you need to say the affirmation again. Please stay with me, because this is the emotional part of the journey – but I promise you you're going to come out on the other side feeling a lot better. So, before we start, let's say it once again, with a bit of modification for clarity:

> "I am the master of my destiny, not a victim of my history. I have the courage to look in the mirror, the humility to say I need help, and the discipline 'to see this process through.'"

WHAT ARE YOUR DISAPPOINTMENTS AND REGRETS?

The big thing you need to do in this step is to identify the disappointments and regrets in the story you've noted down in the previous chapter.

What is it that you regret? Write down those regrets in the worksheet overleaf. Once you are done, I want you to think about why you regretted having done/experienced those situations in the first place and put that in writing as well.

APPRECIATE YOUR PAST

WHAT DISAPPOINTMENTS OR REGRETS DID YOU EXPERIENCE?

What did you regret?	Why did you regret it?

For example, in my past, I regret not having studied enough, not being organised enough, and not standing up for what I believe in. I want you to write them as full sentences. For example, my first two would be:
- I regret <u>not having studied enough</u>.
- I regret <u>not standing up for what I believe in</u>.

- I regret ....
- ... and so on!

Next, write down all the regrets you can bring to mind, and then write why they're important. Just regretting without knowing why means you're never going to learn the lessons that can be gained from those regrets.

For example:
- I regret <u>not having studied enough during my university</u> because <u>it screwed up my grades.</u>
- I regret <u>not standing up for what I believe in</u> because <u>it made me think less of myself.</u>

- I regret ....

  because ....
  ... and so on!

Whatever your regrets are, keep looking for reasons behind them, and keep writing them down. If you feel this is a bit heavy, list three regrets — just three regrets, and with them three reasons *why*.

APPRECIATE YOUR PAST

HOW DID YOUR PAST STRUGGLES SERVE YOU?

Once you are done identifying your regrets and their reasons, it's time to make sense of the ways your past struggles have served you. Here's an example. Let's say one of my struggles was that I went to a university that wasn't great, in a city that wasn't inspiring. That struggle is part of the story I've been telling myself. Okay. But how did it serve me?

Well, I became so hungry for the learning I was unable to get from my university, my city, or my social surroundings that I worked ten times harder than anybody else I knew. I worked at developing myself by reading, taking courses, travelling, and watching videos and DVDs (before there were online courses).

So, guess what? Not being in a setting that made it easy for me to learn has served me by forcing me to become a better and more ferocious learner than most people.

Think about challenges that the COVID-19 pandemic brought about. Some people used the time when work was scarce to reconnect and strengthen their family relationships. Others found themselves having to face the reality of the toxic relationships they had been stuck in and were forced to make some hard decisions they were delaying. Some had to use fitness activities as a way to cope with the stress. Whichever it was, the challenge brought by the pandemic served them in the long term.

I want you to think about such struggles in your life and write them down and write how they serve you, and please, I beg you, do not say they did not. It's impossible for a struggle not to serve you. Do you know why? Remember the Yin and Yang? If you face a situation of struggle and pain, naturally, there has to be another side of the equation holding some value and benefit. In the same way, every struggle also has a positive side to it: a side that served you, that helped you become better.

APPRECIATE YOUR PAST

HOW DID YOUR PAST STRUGGLES SERVE YOU?

Struggle	How it served me

Remember, these exercises work only if you are completely honest in your answers. As I mentioned in the previous chapters, be intuitive, and be as truthful as possible about what you are writing down.

This will help you understand your past better, appreciate it, and embrace it for what it is. It will also help you look for the brighter side.

In the next chapter, we will be talking about the second step of your healing process: Understanding what is holding you back.

But first, say it out loud:

> "I am the master of my destiny, not a victim of my history. I have courage, humility, and discipline."

CHAPTER 5

UNDERSTAND WHAT IS HOLDING YOU BACK

You have nothing to prove
to anyone but yourself

> "What the superior man seeks is in himself;
> what the small man seeks is in others."
>
> —CONFUCIUS

In the last chapter, we talked about appreciating your past for what it is and honouring your struggles for the way they have served you. I hope the worksheets helped you look at your past in a way you haven't done before and have given you a different perspective on your life.

If you are still unsure about it, go back to the chapter and make sure you finish the exercises as honestly as you can, and then move on to this one. In this chapter, you are going to learn about what has been holding you back, keeping you latched onto your trauma and preventing you from moving on with your life. You will identify the things in the past that made you feel a need for acknowledgement. You'll understand whose approval you needed in life and what really mattered.

But before we proceed, I want you to say once again:

> "I'm the master of my destiny, not a victim of my history. I have courage, humility, and discipline."

Yes, it might sound repetative. But, again, I am getting you to do this because I know we are peeling off some heavy emotional layers when we do this work. Trust me: it's not easy. So you need to constantly remind yourself that you are the master of your destiny, not a victim of your history, because we are releasing your history through this process.

WHAT DID YOU FEEL YOU SHOULD HAVE BEEN ACKNOWLEDGED FOR, BUT WEREN'T?

In everyone's life, there are times when we feel we should have been acknowledged or recognised for something we have done or achieved, but nobody cared enough to do so. This drastically affects one's self-esteem and can have quite a number of negative effects if left unchecked.

Think about it. We sometimes have a feeling that we are not being acknowledged enough.

Here are a few instances:
- I should have been acknowledged for being such a great son, daughter, sibling, etc.
- I should have been acknowledged for being such a great friend, supporter, partner, lover, etc.
- I should have been acknowledged for being such an amazing employee, team member, business partner, etc.

The list goes on.

So on the following table, I want you to write down a few of the things you believe you should have been acknowledged for.

In the adjacent column, I want you to write *why* you think you should have been acknowledged for it. What is it that makes you think you should have received recognition? Why did you need that acknowledgement? Should you have been acknowledged as a great son because you needed proof of your father's love? Should you have been acknowledged as a great spouse because you needed your husband or wife to validate your existence? What is it that is making you need and want that acknowledgement in your life? Think hard about it, and whatever the reason is, please make a note of it.

WHAT DID YOU FEEL YOU SHOULD HAVE BEEN ACKNOWLEDGED FOR, BUT WEREN'T?

I should have been acknowledged for:	Because:

THE BATTLE FOR APPROVAL

We all seek approval in life; no one is an exception to that. Since the time we were kids, whenever we do something good, we turn to our parents and say, "Mummy, Daddy! Look at what I did!". And then they appreciate us with words like, "Well done, bravo!".

The root of this external need for approval began in our early childhood, as we began to walk and to navigate the world around us. We would depend on external signals from parents to know what was safe (right) or unsafe (wrong). However, as we grow up, this external dependency becomes problematic as we use family, extended family, friends and then society in general to choose our path with their approval. One day, hopefully, it occurs to us that we are no longer babies; we do not need so much external approval for our survival. If anything, so much unnecessary desire for approval becomes an unconscious and invisible jail that limits our fulfilment and flourishing.

We have been entrenched in seeking approval in life and it's a never-ending need. Now, I'm not saying there's something wrong with this, but it does become problematic when it overtakes your life. I want to give you an exercise to help you understand it better. But before you start working on it, sit for a moment and think: whose approval are you unconsciously looking for in general? Is it your mum? Is it your dad? Is it your siblings? Is it your loved ones? Is it a best friend? Is it a figure you aspire to become like?

I'm not trying to be negative about this; a lot of times we seek approval from people we admire or model ourselves on in a positive

UNDERSTAND WHAT IS HOLDING YOU BACK

way. It makes us feel validated. But ask yourself, what are you trying to prove by getting their approval? Think about it: If you're seeking approval from a parent, you're trying to prove that you're a good son or daughter. If you're seeking approval from a best friend, you're trying to prove that you're cool enough to be their friend. Whatever the reason may be, the need for approval is, in one form or another, is tied to seeking validation.

Once you fill in the first two columns of the exercise, I want you to move to the third column, which is very important. Reflect on how such approval-seeking has manifested in your life. This takes a lot of reflection, thinking, and energy. So make sure you sit with a calm mind to think about these things.

Let me give you an example to make it easier for you. Suppose I were seeking approval from my dad, what would I be trying to prove to him? If my dad valued people who were educated, I guess I'd be trying to prove that I'm smart enough. If this is the case, then the third step would be about the way this desire has been manifesting in my life – like I only choose friends who are intellectual, I will only go to universities that are accredited, and I will only work with people who are well educated.

Everything you seek approval about and everything you try to prove to someone, will manifest some way or other in your life. I want you to reflect on these things and take your time filling in the table on the next page.

EXTERNAL APPROVAL (OR APPRECIATION)

Whose approval were you (unconsciously) trying to seek?	What are you trying to prove?	How has this been demonstrated in your work & life?

UNDERSTAND WHAT IS HOLDING YOU BACK

Are you done with the exercise? You are awesome!

Please understand one thing. You don't have to prove anything to anyone but yourself. Let me repeat that. *You don't have to prove anything to anybody in this world but yourself.* Your life and your journey are between you and yourself, so stop trying to prove yourself to others; stop looking for approval from someone else. Instead, love yourself as you are.

Before we move further, I want you to say: "I love and approve of myself." Please say it loudly. It might be difficult to say it out loud for the first time. But don't worry. Say it to yourself quietly. That's okay too. As you progress you should be able to look yourself in the mirror and say it loudly, and lovingly.

You will be shocked by how difficult people find it to look themselves lovingly in the mirror for a few seconds, let alone say something like "I love you." I promise it will be worthwhile if you give it a go.

FRUSTRATION = EXPECTATIONS − REALITY

There is something we need to understand about frustrations. The reason you are frustrated in life is simply that frustration equals expectation minus reality. It's as simple as that. You expect one thing, but something else happens in reality, resulting in frustration.

I am going to try to help you understand how to resolve this. Trust me, you are going to be able to move forward when you get to Step Three, releasing negative emotional baggage. This will be covered in the next chapter.

Before we move on to the next chapter, please repeat the mantra:

> "I am the master of my destiny, not a victim of my history. I have courage, humility, and discipline."

CHAPTER 6

RELEASE YOUR NEGATIVE EMOTIONAL BAGGAGE

There are no mistakes in life,
only lessons learned

"Thank God I found the GOOD in goodbye."

—BEYONCÉ KNOWLES

Congratulations! We are done with the first two steps. Now you're ready to appreciate your past, honour your struggles, and let go of your need for approval.

In this chapter, you will learn how to release the negative and emotional baggage you have been carrying around, and that has been holding you back all this time.

But you know what to do before we move to Step Three of the healing process. You are right. You need to say out loud,

> *"I am the master of my destiny, not a victim of my history. I have courage, humility, and discipline."*

I promise that repeating these lines will serve you. You cannot say this sentence enough, especially during this process.

Another valuable part of this process is developing an understanding of why we hold on to our pain.

WHY DO WE HOLD ON TO PAIN?

Why do we hold on to our old pain and our old stories? We all do it, by the way. I do it. Everybody does it. But why? I think there are two logical reasons why we hang on to these things. The first reason is that we have invested so much time into our old stories. I mean, they are our life stories, after all. For instance, if I'm 40 years old now and I've been living the same story on and on, there's a lot of time and energy and effort I've invested in building that story.

The second reason we hold on to our stories is that, usually, the people and situatinos in these stories have caused us pain. We believe that if we release these stories, we are releasing the person who did us harm and letting them go. None of us want that. So let me help you resolve that situation.

This is a big moment: a wake-up call before you can move on.

Regarding the first reason above, you have to realise that investing in such an old story once you have lived it, survived it, and gotten past it is not going to serve you anymore. It is going to keep you stuck in survival mode. It stops you from thriving and actually makes your life worse. This is as true physically as it is mentally and emotionally.

THERE ARE TWO KEY REASONS WHY WE HOLD ON TO PAINFUL MEMORIES:

	1	2
Reasons you are holding on	You have invested a lot in that old story, and if you let go of it now, what will that mean for all the previous decisions you made?	Letting go of old pain feels like you are letting the person who did you wrong off the hook.
Realisation needed to move on	Realise that what might have served you back then is probably not serving you now.	Letting go is about you; it will allow you to heal and move on with your life.
How to let go	Just ask yourself: Is this serving me now or is it just sucking my energy and keeping me stuck in the past?	You choose to forgive the person without agreeing with their actions.

FREE YOURSELF BY LETTING GO

The second challenge, which is letting go of the person who did you wrong, involves the realisation that by letting them go, you're not *actually* letting them go. What you're letting go of is *the story of pain* you're keeping at the front of your mind. What happened is in the past and life moves on.

You have to ask yourself a question to be able to release those memories. When it comes to the story, ask yourself this: *"Is holding on to that story still serving me or not?"* If not, then it is better for you to let go and start building a new story. That's what we're helping you do now.

The second point is a tougher one, I'll admit that. But remember this: when I talk about letting go, I don't mean that you're letting go of the person who did you wrong. Because the truth is that you've never actually been holding on to *them*. You're not keeping them in a jail cell with your memory. It's *you*; you're holding yourself in that jail cell of pain and memory.

Ask yourself – is holding on to that pain or memory serving me or is it better to let go of it? More importantly, understand that by letting them go you let go of the memory, but you still have the right to say that it was wrong for them to do what they did. Remember, letting go of the memory does not mean that you agree and approve of what they did to you. Nor does it mean you forget and erase what happened. It means you free yourself and give yourself permission to write a new story.

I got this learning when I was looking into the life of Nelson Mandela. He was a deeply inspiring person.

> "As I walked out the door toward
> the gate that would lead to my freedom, I knew if
> I didn't leave my bitterness and hatred behind,
> I'd still be in prison."
>
> —NELSON MANDELA

Let me be clear, that was a man who spent 27 years in prison. Yet he walked out with this realisation – that he had to let go of the pain and bitterness in that cell. I urge you to do the same. Let go of that pain.

It is essential for us to move forward. I understand that this is easier said than done. It took me a while before I could do it. So please pause for a moment to just reflect on those feelings. It might get emotional. It could even take hours before you can get through it. But it's worth the investment, so take as much time as you want.

If you feel tears coming up that is good! Why? Because crying is a primal emotion. As infants we only knew two kinds of communication modes – laughing or crying. If it felt good we laugh and if it did not we cry. As we grew older, we were taught to suppress these emotions; to laugh without reason is rude and to cry without reason is weak.

So in this process, tap into your inner child and allow yourself to cry.

BEING THE WAY I AM BENEFITS ME

I want you to work on an exercise called 'Being the way I am benefits me'. Here's the thing: you will never do anything unless there's some sort of benefit in it for you.

Look, even if you smoke and you know it's killing you, your brain is wired for your benefit, so why would it let you smoke unless you have ulterior motives for smoking? It could be social agreement, it could be chemical addiction – you feel good when you smoke and your body is getting something positive out of it.

I want you to reflect and ask yourself, "How does it benifit me to be the way i am?

This is similar to the previous exercise of thinking about how your past served you, but now is bringing it into the present – you, your trauma reactions, and your self-protective way of being. How do they benefit you in your current state?

You might be saying, "No, being the way I am doesn't serve me." But you've been like this for a while, right? Then the probability is you do have an underlying benefit to staying the way you are, maybe one you are not conscious of.

Thinking back about the smoking example, if you ask most smokers what's in it for them, they will say something along the lines of: "I know it's not good for me and I should quit," but they don't quit! So there must be underlying benefits. Again, it could be social belonging, which means the smoker will subconsciously not want to quit smoking and lose that underlying benefit. An alternative way to get that benefit would be to find friends who have healthy habits. The person can still find social belonging without being stuck with a negative habit.

I'm just giving you an example; this might not be your story. However, I guarantee you that if you write down how staying the way you are is serving you, at least for now, it will be a major eye-opener. So go ahead and reflect on that a bit.

BEING THE WAY I AM BENEFITS ME

Current benefit	Alternative ways to get that benefit
1.	1.
2.	2.
3.	3.
4.	4.
5.	5.
6.	6.
7.	7.
8.	8.
9.	9.
10.	10.

The next step is to think of alternative ways to get these benefits. For example, if being the way you are benefits you by offering you a chance to take it easy, maybe the alternative way to do that is to schedule time off so you can be refreshed and energised to pursue your passion when it's time to do so.

My promise is that when you do these two steps, a lot is going to shift in your life. Because when you understand that there are other ways for you to get these benefits, there are other ways for you to feel more alive, there are other ways for you to get more fun time, things begin to change.

WHAT PREJUDICES DO YOU HAVE AGAINST CERTAIN CAREERS AND SUCCESSES?

When I started my speaking career, I had a huge prejudice statement in my head; it said "English is not my mother tongue, nor was I educated in a Western university, so how can I ever succeed as an international speaker and author? Such a career is only for native English speakers."

I was limiting my potential for success. Then I read a statistic from the World Economic Forum estimating that around 400 million people speak English as a first language; however, one billion people speak it as a *second* language. That created a mental shift in me. I might potentially do a better job being an international speaker and author with English as a second language – because there was a lot more like me than I thought!

RELEASE YOUR NEGATIVE EMOTIONAL BAGGAGE

The exercise here is about breaking free from any prejudice you have towards success by answering: "How do I do it better?".

My "How do I do it better?" statement became this: "My multicultural background will serve me in delivering international talks that speak to a wide audience, including those who have English as a second language." This statement was one of the mental breakthroughs in my career.

I was once coaching a teenager who was phenomenally passionate about food. He would look at me when I was eating and say, "I know what you're feeling from the wrinkles under your eyes when you put the food in your mouth."

In my world that is a great sign of passion for food, and working with this young man, it was apparent that he would be a great chef. But when his father heard about it he got mad! He said, "Not in a million years would I let my son be a cook. Working in a kitchen is not a man's job." Now, this is not true by any means; some of the greatest chefs in the world are men and they are doing great both in their cooking and as celebrities. Take chef Gordon Ramsay. Aside from being a male chef with successful restaurants around the world, he is a TV celebrity, and his estimated net worth is $220 million.

But in the case of the teenager's father, somewhere along the line in his culture it became a source of shame for a man to cook, and this kept passing from one generation to the next. If a man is so prejudiced against his son's choice, because of a story that his culture and/or community told him, he will keep hammering that belief into the son's head until it becomes the son's story. And the son will give up on his dreams. Imagine what a wasted opportunity that would be.

In the case of this teenager, the prejudice is "Only women belong in the kitchen, a man does not work in a kitchen."

In the 'how do I do it better' section, he might write, "I can be the best male chef, and I'm going to be respected in the community while I'm doing it. My masculinity is not defined by a kitchen; it's defined by how well I do things."

Another great example here is the prejudice a lot of people have towards money and rich people. Somewhere along the line, they were convinced that rich people must be crooks to have made so much money.

So, the dilemma becomes, I want money, but *I am not, and do not want to be, a crook*. So we end up giving up on our money dreams to hold on to our values! When this becomes our story, we will be stuck in our own jail, made from a self-limiting belief regarding money.

In this example, the prejudice would be "Rich people are crooks". In 'How do I do it better?' we might find, "I can generate money while upholding my ethics by being in a sustainable and ethical business."

So go ahead and write the top prejudice statements you have. Next to them, write how you can do it better.

WHAT PREJUDICES DO YOU HAVE TOWARDS CERTAIN CAREERS/SUCCESSES?

Statement	How I can do it better

DIAMONDS ARE MADE UNDER PRESSURE

Everything that has happened has happened for a reason. This includes what you might have viewed as a mistake – because I hope you are coming to understand that you have ulterior motives and gain ulterior benefits from anything you do in life. This is true even if it is done subconsciously. Listen to me when I say this: What you have done is part of the path to your destiny.

I am not here to debate if destiny is set in stone; that is a matter of personal philosophy. But I am sure we can agree that your choices today will impact how your destiny forms tomorrow. So, when you come to see challenges as 'on your way' rather than 'in your way' you will appreciate that such challenges are there to make you grow. Diamonds are made under pressure. The more pressure you've been under in your life, the more of a diamond you become. I know you are one; you just need a little shaping.

IT IS STUPID TO 'FORGIVE AND FORGET'

For sure, forgive and let go of any negative emotions. However let me be clear – I'm not telling you to forget, but just to forgive. Because when you forget, you don't remember the lesson. *Forgive YES, but NEVER FORGET.* Remember the lesson and benefit from it, but don't hold on to the emotion. The lesson is all you need to make the correct decision in future; it's the emotions that mess up your head and confuse your heart. Those emotions bring *feelings* from previous memories into the future, when what you actually need are *facts* to avoid making the same mistake again.

In preparation for letting go of negative emotions I would like to remind you that self-love is key, otherwise the negative emotions will find a fertile ground to grow in again.

Self-love is a big topic that requires a book by itself, however, below is a simple exercise to do at least once before proceeding to the next section of the Anger Healing Letter, though I recommend you do it regularly.

Stand in front of a mirror and read the statement below:

> *It's okay.*
> *You did the best you could with what you were given.*
> *You made mistakes – it's okay, we all do.*
> *I forgive you.*
> *I let go of the disappointments, frustrations, anger, sadness, and depression.*
> *I love you. I forgive you.*
> *I am free to make new choices.*
> *It's today's choices that will define a new tomorrow.*

THE ANGER-HEALING LETTER

Forgive and let go of the emotion.
(Do not forget, learn.)

The next thing I want you to do is to write an anger-healing letter to people who make you furious. This is a very important step in the process of forgiving and healing. Let me guide you through this step by step and then you can fill in the blanks on the worksheet in the following pages.

'Dear...'

Who is the person you feel the most anger towards? It could be a parent. It could be a spouse, a partner, a friend, anybody who you believe hurt you. I want you to write, 'Dear...' and then write their name.

'I was angry that you...'

What did they do to you? Your sentence may go something like this: "I was angry that you *didn't let me pursue my career, my passion, that you hurt me, that you judged me...*" Whatever the reason may be, put it all into writing. This is an emotional process, so while you are writing this, expect to get very emotional.

'It made me feel...'

Express how you felt – *"It made me feel unworthy ... it made me feel judged ... it made me feel doubtful of myself."*

'And this has caused me to...'

What was the result? Examples: *"This has caused me to stop believing in myself"* or *"This has caused me not to pursue my passion"* or *"This has caused me to live a life that always felt wrong."*

Then I want you to write, **"Although, I still remember, and I still do not accept nor agree with your actions, I now choose to forgive you for this."**

It's very important to write this line. You are not releasing that person from any wrongdoing. You are not absolving them of what they did to you. What you are doing is releasing the negative emotion and the negative memory. You don't agree with the action, but you're going to let go of it.

Then I want you to get very specific. For example, *"I forgive you for judging me"*, *"...for treating me badly"*, *"...for not supporting me"*. Whatever the reason, describe it the way you need to describe it.

Next comes this: *"I am in control of my life, and I choose for our relationship to be..."* Then describe the next phase of the relationship: *"...to be full of love... to be full of care... to be full of respect."* Maybe you don't want to love that person? All right, but you can at least have basic respect between you.

The last thing to write is, *"I am healed, and I feel loved, I feel worthy, I feel powerful, I feel committed, I feel strong."* Put in whatever positive affirmations that are going to help you, and then sign your name.

RELEASE YOUR NEGATIVE EMOTIONAL BAGGAGE

ANGER-HEALING LETTER

Dear ....

I was angry that you ....

....

....

....

It made me feel ....

....

....

....

SLINGSHOT

I am in control of my life and I choose for our relationship to be……………………………

_____

_____

_____

_____

_____

_____

_____

_____

_____

_____

RELEASE YOUR NEGATIVE EMOTIONAL BAGGAGE

I am healed and I feel..

....

....

....

....

Love..

....

....

....

....

SLINGSHOT

And this has caused me to..

....

....

....

....

Although I still remember and I still do not accept nor agree with your actions,

I now choose to forgive you for ....

....

....

....

RELEASE YOUR NEGATIVE EMOTIONAL BAGGAGE

I understand that it's not going to be easy to write this letter, so take your time. If you are not in the right frame of mind, take a deep breath, get up, have a walk, but please, please, please do not move to the next step before you write this letter (or more than a letter if you need to). If you find yourself unable to write it, perhaps you need to rewind some of the previous steps. Maybe there is something in Step One or Two that you need to work through. This is the last part of Step Three, and we can't move on if you don't release this anger. If you're still feeling angry, then know that you haven't had the full benefit of the exercises. There are still layers to scrape off and heal through, so please be gentle and loving with yourself; please give yourself a big hug, a pat on the shoulder and take yourself out for a nice treat, you earned it!

Before we go to the next chapter, which talks about learning from the past, I would like to emphasise once again the importance of identifying the benefits in being the way you are, of working with those benefits, of loving yourself and living for yourself, and forgiving the people you are angry at.

As we progress to the next chapter please repeat loudly:

> "I am the master of my destiny, not a victim of my history. I have courage, humility, and discipline."

CHAPTER 7

LEARN FROM THE PAST TO SLINGSHOT INTO THE FUTURE

Turn your lessons into wisdom

> *"The best way to predict your future
> is to create it."*
>
> —PETER DRUCKER

Well done! You have now reached the final step in the process of releasing your emotinoal trauma and emotional baggage.

The first three steps in this healing process were about clearing the past. Now it's about moving forward, this chapter is about turning your lessons into wisdom, so you do not drag the worst of your past into the best of your future.

That's why i got you to say "I forgive, but don't forget." because what you *remember* can be taken and turned into wisdom. You don't want to be hanging on to memory for the sake of it. Instead, you want a learning that will serve by making you a wiser person in life.

LEARN FROM THE PAST TO SLINGSHOT INTO THE FUTURE

TIME FOR SOME REFLECTION

*"Insanity:
Doing the same thing over and over again
and expecting different results."*

—ALBERT EINSTEIN

If you're just going to keep repeating the same decisions means you have not learne your lesson. That is why I want you to do this reflection sheet before we end the healing part of the book.

Use the reflection sheet on the next page to look at everything you've done and how your life has gone so far. What were your plans, dreams, and goals? Reflect on that a little and write down how it has gone so far. Write about what went wrong, what went right, and how you can improve both. Even sometimes it seems that everything in your life has gone wrong, the reality is that many things have gone right. We don't have to set the bar too high at the beginning. It could simply be that you're still alive and able to pick up this book so you can learn and begin to heal yourself today. Trust me when I say that many things have worked for you in your life.

Don't victimise yourself. Instead, think about how you can make those things better moving forward. What have you learned?

I'll give you an example. One of the biggest lessons learned in my life was that blaming people for what goes wrong does not serve me. I'm the one who's paying the price anyway, so I might as well take responsibility for my life.

Finally, ask yourself this: Of the things in your control, what do you need to change to get better outcomes? This is very important because you can only change what you know you can change. You must focus only on the things in your control, not what you *wish* you could change. They need to be things in your control, that you can influence. Most people spend their time obsessing over things they have no control over.

Remember, spend time on what you can change, and accept things that you cannot change.

LEARN FROM THE PAST TO SLINGSHOT INTO THE FUTURE

REFLECTION SHEET

How has your life gone so far? What were your plans, dreams and goals?

....

....

....

....

....

What went right, what went wrong, and how can you improve on it?

....

....

....

....

....

SLINGSHOT

What did you learn?

....

....

....

....

....

....

What do you need to change that is in your control to get a better outcome?

....

....

....

....

....

LEARN FROM THE PAST TO SLINGSHOT INTO THE FUTURE

WHAT IS YOUR STORY NOW?

You have now gone through all the steps involved in the process of healing your past. You have written down your story. You have learned how to accept it, honour your struggles, accept and love yourself, forgive people, and even adopt a different perspective on past or present events. You have just finished the final reflection exercise of the healing section.

Before we end this section, I want you to go all the way back to the preparation step. Remember that story you wrote? Go back to it once again and rewrite it, but now with all the new learning and wisdom in your mind.

I promise you, this story is going to be different if you've done the exercises fully and honestly. As of today, you will feel differently about your life. The example in my case was that I wrote *"I'm a victim."* Now, my story transformed and I write *"Oh my God, I've gone on an adventure around the world and I've learned to be stronger than other people, because of the challenges that I've been through. This has made me more powerful, and I'm more empowered with my life."* It's a totally different narrative.

Although some of the memories in your mind might be the same, it's the *angle* from which you're looking at them that changes the story.

So, how does it feel going through the journey, ending where you started but with a different perspective? Wonderful, right?

I hope you were able to clean out your inner clutter, let go of all the emotional baggage, and learn from your struggles. If you couldn't do this, rewind and rework the exercises until you are ready to completely let go, learn, and move towards a brighter future.

WHAT'S YOUR STORY NOW?

....

....

....

....

....

....

....

....

....

....

LEARN FROM THE PAST TO SLINGSHOT INTO THE FUTURE

HEALING STAGE CONCLUSION

Congratulations! You completed the healing stage of your Slingshot journey, and I'm proud of you for that.

Now go ahead and reward yourself for finishing this section! This isn't just a book. What you have gone through is a deep process of cleaning up things that have been sitting inside you for quite some time. I understand if you feel the need to rewind and do this again once, twice, or even many times. This healing section is an independent module. You can redo it at any point in your life to clear emotional baggage that might accumulate again throughout your life.

But for now, it's time to celebrate, so go ahead and reward yourself for living true to the mantra.

"I am the master of my destiny, not a victim of my history. I have courage, humility, and discipline."

B.
MASTER YOUR MINDSET

THIS MIND MASTERY PROCESS IS FOR YOU IF:

 You want improved self-belief.

 You want to stop procrastinating.

 You want to shift your focus to what matters.

 You want to deal with fear, self-doubt, and excuses.

 You do not want to be overwhelmed with anxiety about the future.

CHAPTER 8

WHY AND HOW TO MASTER YOUR MINDSET

What sets a mediocre person apart
from those who are extremely successful?

> *"When you upgrade your habits, mindset and environment, your life will upgrade"*
>
> —SIMON ALEXANDER ONG - BESTSELLING AUTHOR OF ENERGIZE

Through the first part of this book – Heal Your Past, you've confronted those deeply held beliefs that have formed the underlying story of your life, and you've learned to honour your struggles. Now it's time to use them to create a springboard into your future.

In this section of the book, I will help you Master Your Mindset. I am going to teach you powerful tools and techniques that successful people use. This will get you out of the spiral of self-doubt and shift your mindset to a winning one.

By the time you conclude this section, you will understand the powerful impact your mindset has on your performance, and how it either works with or against your success. You will also learn to use neuro-linguistic methods that help increase your probabilities of success, help you deal with self-doubt, eliminate limiting beliefs, and replace them with liberating truth.

MEDIOCRE PEOPLE VS SUCCESSFUL PEOPLE

Over my years of interviewing some of the world's highest-achieving entrepreneurs, leaders, Olympians, and artists, I found that they all had a differentiating characteristic that makes them stand out from the crowd and enables them to realise their dreams of achieving inspiring results.

The biggest difference between a mediocre person with a passion and a high-achieving person is the way their mind functions and operates. One of the interviews that stands out for me in this context is the one I did with Tasha Danvers, a two-time Olympian and Olympic Bronze Medallist. She said to me:

> *When you get to a certain level, especially something like the Olympic Games, everyone has got talent. What makes the difference between those who make it to the podium, or not, is mental! There was half of a second between me and gold! What made the difference was not physical, it's mental.*

Think of mindset as the operating software of our brains when thinking and making decisions. Ultimately, it is the mindset successful people develop that enables them to achieve greater things. They put aside negative thoughts like doubt, hesitation, and pessimism and train themselves to think of themselves as successful. That turns their problems into challenges and their challenges into opportunities. We spent some time on this in the last section – Heal Your Past – when we spoke about obstacles being lessons 'on the way' and not 'in the way'.

SLINGSHOT

THREE STEPS TO MASTERING YOUR MINDSET AND OWNING YOUR FUTURE

 Believe in yourself.

 Deal with procrastination and self-limiting beliefs.

 Focus on what matters.

 Believe in yourself

This is an issue a lot of people struggle with. Whatever the reason might be, self-belief is one of the hardest things for many people to achieve. Through exercises and contemplation, I'll help you overcome that feeling of self-doubt and empower you with the tools to enhance that ability to believe in yourself through:
- Understanding the power of fear.
- Learning about the Mindset Performance Loops.
- Learning how to manage weaknesses.
- Realising it's never too late.
- Understanding what your 'excuses' are.
- Knowing why to pursue passion.

Deal with procrastination and self-limiting beliefs

We all have a dream to follow or a passion to pursue. But more often than not, procrastination hinders our progress, throwing away everything we work for. Everyone has fallen prey to this demon at least once in their life.

Self-limiting beliefs also pose a threat to our success. In further chapters, I will discuss ways to deal with procrastination, and we will learn about the three different kinds of self-limiting beliefs. We will also look at how the power of gratitude can help us with these issues.

Focus on what matters

We all tend to focus on things that don't really matter. (Think "Social Media" amongst many others.) We tend to shift focus to less meaningful tasks to escape our anxiety or feel a sense of achievement through small wins. This is OK for the short term, but if we do not learn how to put our focus where it should be, then we will never get to our goals. I will teach you how to prioritise your goals and place all your focus and energy in the right place. We do this through:
- Asking the right questions.
- Establishing daily tasks that help achieve our passion.
- Using what we have to get what we want.
- Energy decluttering exercises to allow space for new blessings.

It's simple, right? So why hasn't everyone done it? Why aren't we all living the life of our dreams?

It's because most people don't want to implement change. They don't want to do anything different, yet they want different results. But you aren't like them. You've done Part One of this book and have healed your past. Now let's go master your future. Are you ready?

Awesome! Just go right ahead and flip the page, where we are going to discuss the first tool in developing a successful mindset: Believing in yourself.

Which obviously will require you to say this and believe it:

> "I am the master of my destiny, not a victim of my history. I have courage, humility, and discipline."

A gentle reminder to download your exclusive Empowerment Bonus Pack. Simply go to www.Moustafa.com/Slingshot or scan the QR code below and enter the code PASSION.

Scan this QR to download your bonus pack

CHAPTER 9

BELIEVE IN YOURSELF

Who else will?

> *"It's the lack of faith that makes people shy away from challenges and I believe in myself."*
>
> —MUHAMMAD ALI

I always say, you will never have a life until you believe in yourself. This is something people forget about. We keep hoping in life that people will believe in us.

Guess who has to believe in you first? You! Yes, you are the person who has to believe in you first.

That's something that I remind myself of when I'm looking in the mirror. I BELIEVE IN MYSELF.

And I want you to say to yourself, as loudly as you can, *"I believe in myself!"*.

Let people think you are crazy. It doesn't matter. You know why? Because you are passionate. And passion is fuelled by belief in yourself.

In this chapter, we are going to talk about how fear is an illusion. We are going to uncover the mindset-performance loop and its significance. You will learn how to work towards building an opportunity mindset and eliminating the excuses that hinder you from pursuing your passion.

Are you ready?

THE POWER OF FEAR

"There is no illusion in life greater than fear."

—LAO TZU

Most of the time, fear is much more exaggerated in our mind than it really is in actual life, that is IF it even happens.

Our mind does that as a kind of self-protection mechanism, which is something we discussed in the first section of this book. Saying out loud that you believe in yourself is the first step to overcoming that fear.

Fear is a double-edged sword. It's useful when you're running away from a sabre-toothed tiger (if you've been living in a cave), if you're about to get hit by a car, or if you're about to get mugged, but it's not necessary for everything that you do – especially if you're pursuing your passion. As a little dose of caution, fear is good. It keeps you alert and awake. But when you're engulfed by fear, then life will always look like a war zone. To keep your fear in check, you need to work on your mindset.

I do a lot of extreme sports, including skydiving. Having a healthy level of fear helps keep me alive! It makes me want to triple-check my gear to make sure the parachute will open when it has to and that I follow procedures on every step. But I don't have fear to the extent that it stops me from pursuing my passion for such activities. If anything, excessive fear and/or panic is a big 'no-no' in such sports because it clouds your judgment and causes accidents.

The same logic applies to any fear we create in our mind about any new decision such a changing careers, starting or ending a relationship; so feel the fear and do it anyway.

MINDSET-PERFORMANCE LOOP

Your mindset determines your attitude, and your attitude determines your behaviour. Think about it: If you have a certain mindset towards something, you have a certain attitude towards it, and that attitude determines how you behave. Behaviour translates into action, and action drives results.

Here's where the magic is. When you get great results, your performance is positively impacted. Am I right?

MINDSET-PERFORMANCE LOOP

Mindset → Attitude → Behaviour → Actions → Results → Performance → Mindset

Think about how most of our lives go in waves. At times when our 'mindset' is unbeatable we feel we can win against the odds and life seems to be in flow. We believe we can hit our sales targets, get fit, have a great social life and do whatever we set our minds to. And that ends up being our reality: We do achieve and achieve till we believe we are unbeatable. So our results started in our mind.

On the other hand, when something major happens in the world a global financial crisis, the COVID-19 Pandemic, the threat of a war after the Russian invasion of Ukraine, or whatever, we then suddenly shift into fear. This leads to a lack of self-belief, and so the chain goes on till our performance follows our belief. Again, it all started in the mind.

Those cycles – the virtuous cycle and the vicious cycles – refer to a complex chains of events that reinforce themselves through a feedback loop. A virtuous circle has favourable results, while a vicious circle has detrimental results.

Where does all of this begin? Where does this loop start?

In your mind!

So, it's safe to say that your destiny is written by *you*, based on the thoughts that you keep in your head, consistently over time. This is why I've dedicated an entire chapter towards tackling the negative mindset and implementing the success mindset.

Watch your **THOUGHTS**

For they become **WORDS**
Watch your **WORDS**

For they become **ACTIONS**
Watch your **ACTIONS**

For they become **HABITS**
Watch your **HABITS**

For they become **CHARACTER**
Watch your **CHARACTER**

For it becomes your **DESTINY**

—LAO TZU

MANAGING WEAKNESSES

Some people ask me, "What should I do about my weaknesses?". The answer is very simple. *Focus* on your strength and *manage* your weaknesses. That means you need to bring your weaknesses to an acceptable minimum so they don't cause too much damage in your life. But don't spend the majority of your time trying to fix your weaknesses. If you do, you're wasting the time and energy that could be invested in making your strengths better and better.

You can do so by learning new skills to turn your weaknesses around so they no longer cause too much damage in your life, i suggest you spend only about 10% to 20% on managing weaknesses. The rest of your time should be invested on getting better at things that you love doing so you can become really great at them, this will make you stand out as one of the best and will make you feel great about yourself.

TEMPORARY CONFUSION IS NECESSARY

This journey you're on is the passionate pursuit of your dreams. This means you will be passing through a transformational period, which is going to get very confusing. I guarantee you that. If it is not confusing, then you're probably not being gutsy and daring enough, and not believing in yourself. Why do I say that? Because if you're not a bit confused, it means you're setting goals that are within your comfort zone – you don't need to change your mindset to achieve them. Do this and things will stay the same. You've got to think big – you've got to dream so big that it scares you.

In my work helping people live a passionate life, I ask them to write something I call a 'Passion Statement'. Think of it as a personal version of a company's Mission Statement. The Passion Statement is a one-page document one writes to describe the truly passionate life they want to live. The way I know if somebody is writing a truly genuine passion statement: They're either jumping up and down because they're so excited, or they're so freaked out and inspired that they get tears in their eyes. They have a vision that is way beyond their current reality. They believe in themselves so much that they can see the possibilities without even knowing yet how they will make them happen. You can get a free copy of the Passion Statement template on www.Moustafa.com/Slingshot

Once someone has written their Passion Statement to such an inspiring level, they are bound to go through a phase of confusion. Think of a caterpillar that is transforming into a butterfly. When it's in the cocoon, do you think it's comfortable? It is very uncomfortable for the caterpillar. It is so uncomfortable that the caterpillar dies momentarily before being reborn as a butterfly. This is what you're going through with this book. You are transforming. In a transformation process, a temporary identity crisis is natural. So own it, and accept it as a rebirth for the new, more passionate you.

CHANGE YOUR LANGUAGE, CHANGE YOUR MIND

But how do you deal with this discomfort? Just get comfortable being uncomfortable. To help you do that, we are going to run through some exercises. The first two are based on neurolinguistics.

BELIEVE IN YOURSELF

You might have heard of this by the name of NLP, or NeuroLinguistic Programming. I'm not a big fan of the 'programming' part because it makes people think they can actually program somebody else's mind or totally reprogram their own. Neurolinguistics is about how the use of language impacts the neurology of the brain and thus performance. This is the mindset-performance loop we discussed earlier.

So, for you to change your results, you must change your thoughts. To change your thoughts, you must change the way you describe them in your mind.

Let's look at an example. If I told you I have a "problem", how would you feel? I don't think the majority of people wake up in the morning thinking "Oh! I want to deal with a problem." They wake up in the morning hoping for a better day than yesterday. Now, let's describe the same situation as a "challenge" instead. I come to you and I say I have a challenge for you. How do you feel? My guess is that you would suddenly find a little bit more energy. You're up for a challenge, right? "I can defeat it, I can beat it, I'm powerful, I'm strong!"

You see, just changing the word to 'challenge' calls on a more powerful energy.

Now imagine the same situation once again, but now describe it as an "opportunity." I come to you and say "Hey, I've got an opportunity for you." You're probably going to say "Oh my god! an opportunity." Who does not want an opportunity, especially if you want to live a passionate life?

There's a secret to making this thing work. You have to say it loudly. I want you to say the phrase "I have a problem", then I want to you say "I have a challenge", then I want you to say "I have an opportunity" and notice the changes in your body language when you're saying these words.

Let me give you a practical example to explain this further. I'm sure most of you would know the Leaning Tower of Pisa in Italy. Do you think the people responsible for the tower looked at this as a problem, a challenge, or an opportunity? If you said a problem or a challenge, think again. Because if they saw it as a problem or a challenge, they would have tried to make it straight. And then there would never be the Leaning Tower of Pisa and there would never be any tourism there. It is one of the most visited places in the world. Why? Because it's leaning. Architecturally, it's a disaster, but from a tourism perspective, it's absolutely phenomenal. Over the years engineers have made little fixes to keep the tower from falling over. But they have not tried to straighten it. They've looked at the situation as an opportunity, not as a problem or a challenge.

> *"When the mind is weak,*
> *the situation becomes a problem.*
> *When the mind is balanced,*
> *the situation becomes a challenge.*
> *When the mind is strong,*
> *the situation becomes an opportunity."*
>
> —MOUSTAFA HAMWI

You see that the situation did not change in any of the instances that I described to you. What *has* changed is the strength of your mind. So, make sure you're coming from a strong mindset that enables you to see the opportunity — because when you're feeling weak, you're only going to see the problem.

If you're not quite in the space of seeing the opportunity, at least start by seeing a "challenge" rather than a "problem". You're going to overcome a challenge. But please, please, please, whatever you do, do not use the word 'problem'. I want you to take an eraser to your vocabulary and tell yourself: "The word 'problem' does not exist in my mind." Start erasing it now. When you start describing it as a challenge, it allows you to begin adopting the opportunity mindset.

IT'S NEVER TOO LATE

When I talk about the opportunity mindset, some people tell me, "Listen, it's a bit late for me." I've had people in their late 50s saying, "Listen, isn't it a bit too late for me to pursue my passion?". My answer to them is "No. It's never too late, because you are still alive." Remember this, you are still here, and you have an opportunity to live life on your own terms, starting today. You might not be able to change the past, but you can work towards your future, no matter how old you are.

I might not be able to go back in time and give you back the years of youth, but I can show you examples of people who started late and finished great. Ray Kroc, who is credited with the global expansion of McDonald's, began in his 50s. He started late, yet he never gave up.

Similarly, John Pemberton, who developed a beverage that would later go on to become Coca-Cola, was in his 50s. Colonel Sanders started Kentucky Fried Chicken at 65, and by all measures, his life was a disaster until then, but he never, ever gave up. Now, let me make a small disclaimer here. I am using these as examples of successful businesses; I'm by no means endorsing junk food. I'm very much against junk food. What I'm saying to you is, please, go ahead and pursue your passion, no matter how old or how young you are. It's never too late and it's never too early.

> "Success is going from failure to failure without loss of enthusiasm."
>
> —ABRAHAM LINCOLN

LEARNING VS. FAILING

To help you deal with your fear, do the exercise on the next page. Answer the question, "What's the worst than can happen when I pursue my passion?"

For instance, the first thing you might write is "I'm going to fail." The next thing you might write is "I'm going to lose money" or "My family might not like it". You might be thinking, "My friends might feel that I'm not their friend anymore and I don't belong to them because I'm pursuing a different career and a different life." Mention that too. Keep going and write every single bad scenario you can imagine.

BELIEVE IN YOURSELF

THE **WORST** THAT CAN HAPPEN WHEN I PURSUE MY PASSION:

1. ....

2. ....

3. ....

4. ....

5. ....

6. ....

7. ....

8. ....

9. ....

10. ....

"There is no greater illusion than fear."

—LAO TZU

Now, I have one question for you. **SO WHAT?**

You're going to fail — so what? You start climbing up the ladder again. Because remember, you have only truly failed when you've given up. Until then it's learning. You see, all of these things you've written down are actually not failures. The worst that can happen is that you're going to learn and grow and learn and grow.

Legendary people throughout history have gone through failure after failure. But they used it as a building block to become great and successful.

> *"I have missed more than 9,000 shots in my career. I have lost almost 300 games. Twenty-six times, I have been trusted to make the game-winning shot and I failed over and over and over again. And that's why I succeed."*
>
> —MICHAEL JORDAN

It is important to understand that failed experiences are the building block of success. It's just that most people don't have the stamina and the energy to keep going from one experience to the next until they hit success. They judge themselves as a 'failure' too quickly — rather than as someone who has simply gone through a failed experience.

> *"Every battle is won before it is ever fought."*
>
> —SUN TZU, THE ART OF WAR

So how do you get past this first mindset hurdle and reframe failure? All you have to do is write that list of 'the worst that can happen' and then get over it. It's that simple! Once you understand the fear is in your head, dealing with it in real life is much easier.

WHAT'S YOUR EXCUSE?

Now, let's do another exercise. We all have excuses unique to ourselves. We have excuses that are common to others as well. The most common excuses I hear are "I don't have time," or "There's the kids," or "I don't have money," "I'm too young," "I'm too old." It's funny, you know: The young ones say I'm too young, the old ones say I'm too old, and those in the middle say "Not now; I'll do it later." The point is they're all excuses.

On the "excuses" sheet on the next page I want you to write down the most common excuses you use when you do not want to do something. I know you have some, as much as I do and everyone else does.

THE MOST COMMON **EXCUSES** I USE:

1. ....

2. ....

3. ....

4. ....

5. ....

6. ....

7. ....

8. ....

9. ....

10. ....

> "The only thing standing between you and your goal is the bullshit story you keep telling yourself as to why you can't achieve it."
>
> —JORDAN BELFORT

Let me explain why we're doing this exercise. Now you've written them down, the next time you catch yourself using one of these excuses, you're going to turn to this page. When you look at that same sentence you've just used, you're going to realise that this was an excuse made up out of fear. You're going to say, "No. This is an excuse. I know that now."

I'm so inspired by a man called Juan José Méndez. He is a Spanish Paralympic cyclist. He does not have a left leg or a left arm. If a man missing a leg and an arm can get out of bed every single morning and get on a bicycle to train, day in and day out until he becomes an Olympian, what is your excuse?

Carmenabella from https://commons.wikimedia.org/

From now on, I hope you're not going to use any more of these excuses, because they are just that, excuses, and they are stopping you from living a truly passionate life. Understand that when you have big enough 'whys', the 'hows' are going to take care of themselves.

WHY PURSUE YOUR PASSION?

Take a moment to yourself and think about this: Why do you want to pursue your passion? You have just noted your excuses and you have thought about the failure. Now I want you to think of it from the other perspective. What's the best that can happen? Here are some examples:

1. You will succeed.
2. You're going to achieve your dream.
3. You're going to become free.

Please keep going. I'm just prompting you, I want you to write 10–12 points. If there's anything more important than the sheet of excuses you wrote and the sheet of the worst scenarios, it's this one. I want you to realise how many benefits you're going to get by pursuing your passion. They definitely outweigh the worst-case scenario. Once you see that, the probability of your pursuing it fully is going to become larger and larger.

Take all the time you need and keep writing as much as possible. The more reasons you write, the more your motivation level increases.

BELIEVE IN YOURSELF

THE BEST THAT CAN HAPPEN WHEN I PURSUE MY PASSION:

1. ....

2. ....

3. ....

4. ....

5. ....

6. ....

7. ....

8. ....

9. ....

10. ....

"Focusing on the best possible outcomes increases the possibility of the best happening."

—MOUSTAFA HAMWI

THE TOP 5 REGRETS

An article in *The Guardian*[2] told the story of Bronnie Ware, an Australian nurse who spent several years working in palliative care, caring for patients in the last 12 weeks of their lives. She recorded their dying epiphanies in a blog called Inspiration and Chai, which gathered so much attention that she put her observations into a book called *The Top Five Regrets of the Dying*.

Number 5 was "I wish I had the courage to express my feelings." So, if you love somebody and you haven't told them, please go ahead. Go back to your parents, to your loved ones, your spouses, your children, tell them how much you love them.

Number 4 was "I wish I had let myself be happier." It's notable that they said *let myself* be happier because, as I mentioned, happiness is a choice. It's something that's up to you; you don't need to pursue it.

Number 3 was "I wish I had stayed in touch with my friends." Do you know why they say that? Because when you're on your deathbed, you're not going to have your work chasing you. You're not going to have the bank standing by, telling you "Oh, we're going to miss you." It's the people you care for and the people who care for you who are going to be there for you on your deathbed.

---

2   https://www.theguardian.com/lifeandstyle/2012/feb/01/top-five-regrets-of-the-dying.

Number 2 was "I wish I hadn't worked so hard." I believe people say this because they were not working on something truly passionate to them, so they felt like they slaved their lives away. Hopefully, by doing what you're doing now, you're going to be working on something you're truly passionate about.

On top of the list, Regret Number 1 for dying people was this: **"I wish I had had the courage to live a life that was true to myself. Not a life that others expected of me."** Contemplate that. Is that what you want your status to be? Do you really want to reach the end of your life and say I regret not living the life I wanted?

Let's do another exercise. On the next page write down all the regrets you'll have if you *don't* follow your passion.

IF I DON'T PURSUE MY PASSION I WILL **REGRET:**

1. ....

2. ....

3. ....

4. ....

5. ....

6. ....

7. ....

8. ....

9. ....

10. ....

> "Regret for the things we did can be tempered by time; it is regret for the things we did not do that is inconsolable."
>
> —SYDNEY J. HARRIS

Even after doing all these exercises, if you still have doubt, just remember this: No matter how long you're going to live, eventually we all die. If you were about to die, what would you regret about not pursuing your passion?

I would regret not being free, not living a truly passionate life. I want you to write all of these regrets on your list, because this is a kind of fear that I *want* you to have. This is the fear that is going to motivate you to pursue your passion.

In the next chapter, we will look at the most common excuses that hinder people from pursuing their passion, and we will learn how to overcome self-limiting beliefs.

So go ahead and say the mantra before flipping the page:

"I am the master of my destiny, not a victim of my history. I have courage, humility, and discipline."

CHAPTER 10

DEAL WITH PROCRASTINATION AND SELF-LIMITING BELIEFS

The Monkey Ladder

> *"Do just once what others say you can't do, and you will never pay attention to their limitations again."*
>
> —JAMES COOK

As humans, we all have beliefs. These beliefs can be about anything. They can be about the world, the people around us, the way we live, and even about ourselves. As much as our beliefs can help us when we have the right ones, not every belief drives us to goal attainment! Many of our beliefs can be limiting.

In this chapter, I want to talk to you about limiting beliefs and how to deal with them. Why are they called limiting 'beliefs'? To start with, they are just "beliefs", not facts. Our minds make them as real as can be, but they start mostly in our heads. Over time, they can start ruling our lives, if we let them, by becoming self-fulfilling prophecies.

There are two types of beliefs. There are beliefs that free you and there are beliefs that limit you. The good news is that since they start as beliefs in our heads, we can change them from 'limiting' to 'freeing' by using a simple and practical process. But first, let's understand why such beliefs occur.

THE 'MONKEY LADDER'

An article in *Psychology Today*[3] described an experiment involving five monkeys, a ladder, and a banana. Descriptions of this experiment can also be found in various blogs, books, and speeches. This is how author and Creativity Expert Michael Michalko described the experiment in his blog post.

> *This human behavior of not challenging assumptions reminds me of an experiment psychologists performed years ago. They started with a cage containing five monkeys. Inside the cage, they hung a banana on a string with a set of stairs placed under it.*
>
> *Before long, a monkey went to the stairs and started to climb towards the banana. As soon as he started up the stairs, the psychologists sprayed all of the other monkeys with ice-cold water. After a while, another monkey made an attempt to obtain the banana. As soon as his foot touched the stairs, all of the other monkeys were sprayed with ice-cold water. It wasn't long before all of the other monkeys would physically prevent any monkey from climbing the stairs.*

---

3   https://www.psychologytoday.com/au/blog/games-primates-play/201203/what-monkeys-can-teach-us-about-human-behavior-facts-fiction.

Now, the psychologists shut off the cold water, removed one monkey from the cage, and replaced it with a new one. The new monkey saw the banana and started to climb the stairs. To his surprise and horror, all of the other monkeys attacked him. After another attempt and attack, he discovered that if he tried to climb the stairs, he would be assaulted.

Next, they removed another of the original five monkeys and replaced it with a new one. The newcomer went to the stairs and was attacked. The previous newcomer took part in the punishment with enthusiasm!

Likewise, they replaced a third original monkey with a new one, then a fourth, then the fifth. Every time the newest monkey tried to climb the stairs, he was attacked. The monkeys had no idea why they were not permitted to climb the stairs or why they were beating any monkey that tried.

After replacing all the original monkeys, none of the remaining monkeys had ever been sprayed with cold water. Nevertheless, no monkey ever again approached the stairs to try for the banana. Why not? Because as far as they know that's the way it's always been around here.

A small note worth mentioning is that this experiment probably did not happen as described, however recent experiments conducted by scientists in several credible universities have shown similar results of "herd behaviour" – so this story can still teach us something about ourselves. It gets you to simply ask where in your life you started adopting limiting beliefs. They may have been passed on to you, after being accepted for generations, without you even asking, "Why am I even doing that?".

If you want to grow, take the lid off your head, because that lid is closed and it's rusty and it has a lot of old limiting beliefs. When you get rid of your limiting beliefs and replace them with liberating truth, you're going to feel a lot freer and a lot more powerful.

THREE DIFFERENT CATEGORIES OF LIMITING BELIEFS

 Limiting beliefs about the world: These are big limiting beliefs that relate to the world overall.

 Limiting beliefs about others: These are about people that you interact with.

 Limiting beliefs about yourself: These are about your own capabilities and value.

Think about these three types of limiting beliefs – about the world, about others, and about ourselves. Combined, they can literally destroy the probability of your living a passionate life. But don't worry, we're going to solve them one by one. Before we get started, I want you to think about something Henry Ford said: "Whether you think you can or whether you think you cannot, you are right."

On the coming pages I will get you to do an exercise, 'For me to achieve my passion, I believe that'. This is about adopting new beliefs – beliefs about the world. What limiting beliefs do you have about the world?

A good example of limiting beliefs comes from the 1950s, when African-Americans were forced to ride in the back of buses and were frequently ordered to surrender their seats to white people. One day Rosa Parks was arrested for her refusal to surrender her seat to a white person. On December 5, 1955 – the next Monday – the Montgomery Bus Boycott started, and that was the beginning of the end for such racial segregation.

Rosa Parks challenged the idea of racial inequality. It was not true, right, or just. It was just a limiting belief, when she broke it she rewrote history.

Martin Luther King once said "I have a dream." He saw a limiting belief that was impacting other people and he decided to challenge that belief. He set it as a dream and as a goal, and he worked for it. So, I want you to write down the limiting beliefs that you have about the world. Then I want you to write what the actual truth is. What is the liberating truth that's going to change that mindset for you?

Here's another example. Your limiting belief might be: "I believe the world does not support women being executives or fully breaking

DEAL WITH PROCRASTINATION AND SELF-LIMITING BELIEFS

the glass ceiling." A liberating truth would be: "I am a powerful woman who is going to be able to go out there and compete in the corporate world and win. I can become better than everybody else because I have the ability to do what anyone else can do, and do it even better." I believe you can do it.

Write a couple of limiting beliefs you hold about the world. The next thing I want you to write is a list of limiting beliefs about others. These are things that you believe others are going to hold or use against you. It might be related to your community or your society. So, in the case of the teenager who wanted to be a chef, his limiting belief was: "If I follow my passion for food my father is going to disown me, because it isn't a masculine role in his eyes." This is directly related to the young man's father. What would be the liberating truth? "I can be a chef and my father will still love me and be proud of my success."

I know this food example might not relate to you, but I'm offering it as a prompt. Write down the limiting beliefs you have that involve the opinions of others.

Third, I want you to write down limiting beliefs about yourself. Have you ever caught yourself thinking or saying, "I'm not good enough... I can't do this... I don't like this"?

After writing my Passion Statement I heard myself saying "Who am I to be an inspirational speaker?", "Who am I to be a coach?", "Who am I to change the world?", "Who am I to be an author?", "Who am I to make an impact on this planet?" These are all possible limiting beliefs about one's self.

What is yours? Do you believe you don't have the skills? Or that you don't have the talent or determination? That you are weak or not good enough? Whatever it is, write that limiting belief. The liberating truth will be something like this: "I am good enough as I am. I am determined enough to get to where I want to be. I am strong enough. I can, because I choose to believe that I can."

Pause your reading at this point, and take time to do this exercise. I want you to understand that you can break free when you replace your limiting beliefs with liberating truth. Because the truth will set you free.

DEAL WITH PROCRASTINATION AND SELF-LIMITING BELIEFS

FOR ME TO ACHIEVE MY PASSION I **BELIEVE** THAT:

About The World

Limiting Belief ....

Liberating Truth ....

Limiting Belief ....

Liberating Truth ....

About Others

Limiting Belief ....

Liberating Truth ....

Limiting Belief ....

Liberating Truth ....

About Myself

Limiting Belief ....

Liberating Truth ....

Limiting Belief ....

Liberating Truth ....

> "Whether you think you can, or you think you can't, either way you are right."
>
> —HENRY FORD

POWER OF GRATITUDE

Let's now talk about gratitude a little bit, because gratitude is important if you want to have a different outlook on life.

An article by Harvard Medical School titled "Giving thanks can make you happier"[4] states that

> in positive psychology research, gratitude is strongly and consistently associated with greater happiness. Gratitude helps people feel more positive emotions, relish good experiences, improve their health, deal with adversity, and build strong relationships.
>
> Two psychologists, Dr Robert A Emmons of the University of California, Davis, and Dr Michael E McCullough of the University of Miami, have done much of the research on gratitude. In one study, they asked all participants to write a few sentences each week, focusing on particular topics.

---

4   https://www.health.harvard.edu/healthbeat/giving-thanks-can-make-you-happier.

DEAL WITH PROCRASTINATION AND SELF-LIMITING BELIEFS

One group wrote about things they were grateful for that had occurred during the week. A second group wrote about daily irritations or things that had displeased them, and the third wrote about events that had affected them (with no emphasis on them being positive or negative). After 10 weeks, those who wrote about gratitude were more optimistic and felt better about their lives. Surprisingly, they also exercised more and had fewer visits to physicians than those who focused on sources of aggravation.

We all – myself included – go through life taking things for granted. We take it for granted that we can wake up every morning and get out of bed and get on with life. But that is not the case for a lot of people out there. Joel Whitwell is the author of *One Eye One Ear – No Worries: A Story of Resilience*. He was born with a craniofacial deficiency leaving him with only one ear and one eye; simply put, he was born with half a face. I have spoken with him personally a few times and he is genuinely full of gratitude for everything he has, rather than being upset about what he does not have. This makes him an inspiring character, rather than a limited one.

I want you to write down a list of things you're grateful for. I've written the first thing for you – being able to access this book and work on your mindset. Isn't this something to be grateful for?

Go ahead and write at least 12 things you are grateful for, and if you want to feel better about your life, do a gratitude list every day.

This is an exercise that will transform the way you perceive life and the way you act every day.

If you can't find at least 10–12 things, my guess is that you've probably taken things in your life for granted. Maybe it's worth pausing a little bit here and reflecting on how grateful you should be simply because you're alive. That alone could engender a long gratitude list below it.

DEAL WITH PROCRASTINATION AND SELF-LIMITING BELIEFS

I AM **GRATEFUL** FOR:

1 Having this book to help me on my journey

2.

3.

4.

5.

6.

7.

8.

9.

10.

"An attitude of gratitude brings abundance into your life."

—MOUSTAFA HAMWI

You may be asking what this has to do with the process of mastering your mindset. Well, if you kept giving presents to someone who is never happy with your generosity, would you keep doing it? If you are not grateful for what the universe offers you, then it will redirect these resources to someone who appreciates them and utilises them.

> *"Acknowledging the good that you already have in your life is the foundation for all abundance."*
>
> —ECKHART TOLLE

Once you're done, say the mantra and flip to the next page, where we will be talking about the last step in the mind mastery process: how to place your focus on what really matters.

> *"I am the master of my destiny, not a victim of my history. I have courage, humility, and discipline."*

CHAPTER 11

FOCUS ON WHAT MATTERS

Where attention goes, energy flows

> *"Where attention goes, energy flows."*
>
> —JAMES REDFIELD, *THE CELESTINE PROPHECY*

If you're going to focus your attention on things that are not working for you, guess what's going to happen? Your *energy* is going to flow towards those very things. Let's go back to the earlier chapters where I talked about focussing on your strengths and managing your weaknesses. I am emphasising this because I don't want you to waste your energy on your weaknesses. Instead, I want you to treat your energy as an investment in your strength and understand that when you focus your energy on what is working, you will achieve better results.

In this chapter, we will learn about asking the right questions and channelling your focus to things that truly matter – to optimise results and achieve success.

ASK THE RIGHT QUESTIONS

There was a point in my journey when I was doing my best and things were not working out. I kept asking myself "What am I doing wrong?".

I would find out what I was doing wrong and fix it. Then I would go to the next wrong thing and fix that as well. I would keep doing it again and again, every single day, until one day I woke up and thought to myself "Maybe I'm asking the wrong question."

"The quality of your life is based partly upon the quality of the questions you ask yourself daily."

—DR JOHN DEMARTINI

Well, I was asking myself the wrong question. I was asking myself what I was doing wrong and I was always finding the answer. Why? Because there's *always* something wrong.

However, the minute I changed my question to "What am I doing right? What do I have at my disposal to increase my probabilities of success?", things started shifting for me.

Look at the activity sheet on the next page. "How is your current situation helping you in achieving your goals?" – this is a powerful question. I'll tell you why. Being passionate is about being resourceful. Nobody's going to hand you your passion on a plate. You're going to have to go and build it up piece by piece, bit by bit, dot by dot, pixel by pixel, second by second. You're going to have to *make* it; it's the masterpiece of *your life*.

You're going to have to be resourceful, grabbing assets from everything around you. Event having fresh air around you is a resource. The book in your hands is an asset. When you get into this mindset of being highly resourceful, the magic will manifest.

Write a list of ways that your current situation is helping you achieve your passion. Let's say you're stuck in a job that you hate. Is the job helping you? If you're telling me no, then perhaps you're not being appreciative of what you have, or not able to use what you have to get what you want, because at least you know you have a steady job. "I'm in a house." "I have access to a lot of friends who love me and care for me." "I'm in a safe country." These are all aspects of your current situation. Start writing how your current situation is helping you achieve your passion.

FOCUS ON WHAT MATTERS

HOW IS YOUR **CURRENT SITUATION** USEFUL IN ACHIEVING YOUR PASSION?

1. ....

2. ....

3. ....

4. ....

5. ....

6. ....

7. ....

8. ....

9. ....

10. ....

"Where attention goes, energy flows."

—JAMES REDFIELD, THE CELESTINE PROPHECY

DAILY TASKS THAT HELP ACHIEVE YOUR GOALS

Now we're going to break down every daily task you are doing and correlate it to your goals. Here's how you're going to do that. Let's say one of the daily tasks you hate is making phone calls. You're in sales and you hate being in this job. Every single day you pick up the phone to make phone calls and you're asking yourself, "How is this going to help me achieve my passion?" Well, you just need a bit of creative thinking. On the left side of the sheet, write the task, 'making sales calls'. Then ask how is this helping you achieve your passion? Think about it using the opportunity based mindset we discussed. Wouldn't you have to make these calls if you were trying to start a business of your own?

If we were to move away from business and look at a different pursuit, we could use the same strategy. Let's say you want to work as an artist, or perhaps a speaker or coach, or maybe you want to do what I'm doing. Guess what? Even I have to make these calls every single day. I have to call the people who help me with my work, I have to call my clients. Isn't this helping my passion?

So, when you start linking the tasks you do not enjoy as much to the actual skills needed for your passion, then you will see things differently. The tasks you hate the most are probably the ones that are serving you the most.

Let's say you are dreaming of opening a restaurant but find yourself in a sales job right now. You may ask how making sales calls serves your love for food! It may not directly help with cooking, but it surely helps you learn how to get clients, which is something you will need when you have your own business. In whatever you do, you will need to 'sell yourself'. Doing sales work teaches you how to tell your story in a way that makes people buy what you have to offer.

One of the people I was coaching had a dream to open a motorbike workshop. However, at that time he was working as a project manager in a marketing agency. After thinking he realised that learning project management will be a core skill he needs once he has saved enough and is ready to launch his workshop. The salary he is getting paid allows him to save for that dream.

Another example I will give you comes from one of my workshops. A gentleman, let's call him Sam, said he loved classic cars but was working in a business development role that required him to do a lot of proposal writing. Now, that seems to be an even more complicated situation than the previous example. However, when we brainstormed a bit he realised that one of the key requirements of handling classic cars is attention to detail, which is also necessary when working on proposals. Since then, he thinks of every proposal as a chance to sharpen the attention to detail he will need when he starts handling his classic cars.

So, remember, everything you are doing is serving you. Now it is time to put on your resourceful thinking cap and finish this exercise.

HOW ARE MY **DAILY TASKS** HELPING ME ACHIEVE MY GOALS?

Task	How is the task helping you get to your goal?	Goals & Passions

"The moment you realize you already have everything you're looking for, the universe gives it to you."

—JOHN F. DEMARTINI

USE WHAT YOU HAVE TO GET WHAT YOU WANT

Once you are done with the above worksheet, I want you to think about this question: What resources do I currently have that will help me achieve my passion?

This is a magical exercise, and definitely one of my favourites. It is something I did when I was feeling at the lowest point of my life. I was almost broke after coming back from India, or at least I thought so till I did this exercise. I wasn't anywhere close to achieving the success I wanted. I had just let go for a lot business opportunities to pursue my dream of talking about passion and helping people connect with their purpose in life. Nothing was working as planned and there I was, looking around me and thinking, "I have nothing left. How am I ever going to achieve my goal?". I grabbed a piece of paper and a pen, and I started writing down everything that I thought could be a resource. And, oh my God! I cannot tell you how many resources I found.

Here's how you're going to do the worksheet:

1. Put a list of all the resources you have on the left side.
2. Put a list of your goals or passions on the right side.
3. Now play a connect-the-dots game, simply think "How can I use this resource to get me to my goal?".

I know it looks a little bit like the previous exercise, but the previous one was generic, whereas this one is specific. The previous one was more about "tasks and activities", but this one is about the "things" that are around you.

Suddenly, I began realising that there were many things around me that I could use in pursuing my passion. I started thinking: "What else do I have? ... Oh my God, I'm sitting at a computer. A lot of people don't have that ... I've got Wi-Fi at home. I don't have to sit in a coffee shop ... I've got 3G on my mobile". Believe me when I say this, once I had written down about four pages of things, my energy went through the roof, because I realised, "I'm so full of resources. I can make this happen".

I promise, just adopt this exercise — just this one worksheet — and a lot in your life will begin to change. What are you waiting for? Go ahead and fill out at least one page. If you can't manage it, you're not looking deeply enough. Don't tell me you don't have resources. Again, if you're sitting at a computer or reading this on your Kindle, that's already a good start. You've got electricity, enough money to buy a phone with a PDF reader on it or a laptop, or even to pay for the rental of a laptop. These things are big advantages if you use them! I don't care where you are in life. I promise you, you've got enough to do this, so go ahead and complete this worksheet.

WHAT **RESOURCES** DO I CURRENTLY HAVE THAT WILL HELP ME ACHIEVE MY PASSION?

Resource	How can I use it to help me get to my goal?	Goals & Passions

"Use what you have to get what you want."

—MOUSTAFA HAMWI

ALLOW SPACE FOR NEW BLESSINGS

Last but not least, to be able to achieve a passionate life, you need to do a bit of lifestyle designing. One of the key elements of lifestyle design is simplifying and decluttering.

> *"Don't be afraid to give up the good for the great."*
>
> —JOHN D. ROCKEFELLER

Here's the interesting thing: When I was going through my journey, I looked at that quote once and I thought, "What do you *mean*, give up the good for the great?". I mean, I've got nothing to give up. And why should I give up the good for the great? Give me the good and I'm going to be happy. I don't need the great." At that point I realised that maybe, just maybe I'm not looking at things the right way. I started drilling down, using something similar to the next worksheet, which is about allowing space for new blessings.

Here's the magic – allowing space for new blessings requires a little decluttering. It means letting go. Sometimes it's things you have or tasks that you do, and sometimes it's even people. This might sound crazy. You might be wondering why you have to let go of certain people in your life. But let me ask you something. How many people can you deal with in your life? You are going to have to let go of some people to make room for new people to come into your life. So, think about a thing, a person or a task. Use your intuition as you do this. Go with your gut feeling. There is often wisdom hidden in that.

Then I want you to write down how much of your time, energy, effort, or money it/they take(s) from you on a weekly, daily or monthly basis. When you get good at it, you start looking by the minute. I'm at the point right now where I start saying, "How long or how much does this take from me on a daily basis, per minute?". I'm counting minutes because when you get so passionate, you don't want to waste a minute of your life.

Next, write down how much time you are going to reduce it to. So, let's say you have a task, something that you have to do – for example, Facebook. I know we love social media, but do we really need to spend a couple of hours a day on it? So, write 'Facebook'.

- How much does it take from me a day? It takes about two hours a day.
- Reduce it to one hour.
- What am I going to do with that extra hour? I'm going to start pursuing X, Y, Z, which is my passion.

So, start writing. Keep thinking of other ways you can trim down the clutter so you can start packing your day with the things you *want* to spend your time on – things that move you towards your dream.

When you do this exercise, I promise you, you will get no less than one more day back on your calendar. I'm not joking. One full working day. Because I know most people (including me until recently), waste time on things that do not matter, but we don't *account* for them. When you do this exercise, you're going to suddenly think:

"Hold on, I've got an hour here I've got 50 minutes there, 15 minutes there, 30 minutes there," and suddenly you've got about eight to nine hours extra. If I give you eight or nine hours a week, do you promise me you're going to use it to pursue your passion? Well, this is the exercise that's going to do it for you.

> **"Life's too short to hang out with people who aren't resourceful."**
>
> —JEFF BEZOS

Before we get to the end, let's talk quickly about the second part of the first column of the worksheet – the people. You see, we all have friends and we all love our friends. However, sometimes we outgrow our friends and we outgrow our surroundings. I mean, we have passions and dreams and they have passions and dreams. Nobody's right or wrong when it comes to dreams; it's their dream.

But if I want to go right and somebody wants to go left, maybe it's time for us to part ways, or spend a little bit less time together so each of us can get to their destination. Accept that this isn't an a traumatic end to a friendship. It's an acknowledgement that you are on different pages and in different stages of your life, and so the direction of your time and energy needs to change. If not, well, you become the average of the people who you spend time with.

TO **ALLOW SPACE** FOR NEW BLESSINGS TO COME INTO MY LIFE, I WILL LET GO OF:

Task/Person	Current time/energy/money spent on it	Reduce it to	This helps me to

"Don't be afraid to give up the good to go for the great."

—JOHN D. ROCKEFELLER

So you might write a person's name and say, "I spend five hours a week with this person but I don't feel this is fulfilling my passionate life. It fulfils that person's agenda." You realise that you keep that person entertained, but you're not entertaining your dream, so reduce it to three hours. You've just gained two hours you can use for your passion.

Over the years I have seen people who do this exercise diligently get back up to a full working day a week, that is about 52 working days a year, close to two months' worth of working time. Ask yourself what amazing things you can achieve with that extra time.

That is one of my personal favourite exercises. I do it at least once a quarter to help me get the most Return On Investment from my schedule.

AND WE ARE DONE!

Congratulations on completing the Master Your Mindset section and staying with me as I guided you on how to shift your mindset.

If you have completed the exercises carefully and truthfully, then I assure you that you are a lot closer to mastering your mindset and pursuing your passion. You are that much closer to becoming the successful person you've always dreamed of being.

I hope you grasp the impact of your mindset on your success and the importance of using neurolinguistics to increase the probabilities of success. You have learned how to deal with fear, self-doubt and excuses, learned to replace limiting beliefs with liberating truth, and learned how to believe in yourself.

I also hope that you have applied my favourite exercises, utilising resources to live a passionate life and decluttering your schedule. So well done.

By now I think you are vibrating the mantra:

> "I am the master of my destiny, not a victim of my history. I have courage, humility, and discipline."

CONCLUSION

DID I REALLY RELEASE MY PAST AND MASTER MY MINDSET?

Keep brushing your teeth

> *"Passionate people do not wait for life to happen to them; they happen to life."*
>
> —MOUSTAFA HAMWI

Firstly, congratulations on completing the book. Please take a moment to honour yourself, give yourself a big pat on the back and go reward yourself. You deserve it!

DID I REALLY RELEASE MY PAST AND MASTER MY MINDSET?

I said in the introduction that this book will *not* help you unless you are serious about making a change in your life. Well, you have invested money, time, and effort to reach the end of this book and do the exercises. In doing so, you have taken the first step towards living the most passionate life ever.

Trust me when I say that you are ahead of most of the people out in this world. Kudos to you for that!

In this book we went through two key stages:

In Stage One we took a step back to heal your past trauma by honouring your past and valuing your struggles. You understood what is holding you back, releasing the negative emotional baggage, and we learned from the past how to move to the future.

And then in Stage Two we helped you master your mindset to own your future, using tools to strengthen your self-belief, deal with procrastination and self-limiting beliefs, and focus on what matters.

With that, I hope I have delivered on my promise to help you release your past and master your mindset by the time you finished this book.

KEEP BRUSHING YOUR TEETH

That being said, releasing the past and mastering your mindset is an ongoing process; it is not just a one-time thing. If you think about it, this book is like going for teeth whitening at the dentist – but you still have to brush your teeth daily. The great thing about the exercises you've learned here is that they can serve both functions. You do the *whole* process now and then, and you can just use specific exercises to help you deal with specific challenges in life if and when they pop up.

As mentioned, I've curated an exclusive Empowerment Bonus Pack that's consistently updated with extra tools, empowering you to live your most passionate life.

Claim yours now at www.Moustafa.com/Slingshot or scan the QR code below and enter the code PASSION."

On a separate note, I would love to hear any feedback you have; you can find my contact info in the Author Bio section after this conclusion.

Scan this QR to download your bonus pack

 LET'S PARTY

If there's one thing I have learned from my previous businesses, it is that you cannot have a party alone. We go through our lives surrounded by people of all kinds. When you live a truly passionate life, you will not be alone. You will attract your own passion tribe.

These are truly passionate people making their money doing what they love while changing the world. They are people on the same journey who understand your struggles and your pain and share their knowledge and their resources. They support and cheer each other on.

These are also people who will hold you accountable on this journey. They will hold your hand and go together with you to inspire the world and live an inspiring life. You are going to build your own Passion Tribe, a network of like-minded people who are on a similar journey.

If you flip further along in this book you will see a section that includes more info on how I can help you on your journey of becoming a global thought leader to spread your passion and purpose to the world.

For now, remember always that you are the master of your destiny, not a victim of your history. You have courage, humility, and discipline.

Moustafa Hamwi
Bestselling Author, International Speaker, and Mindset Coach.
Hypnotherapist, Yoga and Meditation Teacher.

WANT
MORE
HELP IN
MASTERING
YOUR
DESTINY?

ABOUT THE AUTHOR

Moustafa Hamwi

Here to help you Win The Game Of Work, And Business Of Life

Moustafa is a bestselling author, international speaker, and mindset coach.

Moustafa's diverse expertise encompasses a successful corporate career, serial entrepreneurial ventures, a solid coaching education, and a variety of adventure sports experiences.

His quest for self-discovery regularly leads him to learning and meditation centres worldwide, exploring the intricacies of mind, body, and soul.

Moustafa's distinctive lifestyle as an executive nomad has seen him traversing the globe, often spending months living out of a campervan, immersing himself in diverse cultures while forging a deep connection with nature.

His work focuses on empowering leaders and teams to cultivate mental wellbeing through mindset mastery, freeing them from negative cycles and reconnecting them to passion and purpose

Curious to learn more? Visit www.Moustafa.com and embark on a journey of mastering your destiny.

ABOUT THE AUTHOR

Below are some of Moustafa's relevant credentials

Professional Qualifications
- Executive Coaching Certificate – Marshall Goldsmith, Stakeholder Centered Coaching
- Executive Coaching Certification – Sherpa Institute
- Diploma of Yoga Teaching – Australian Yoga Academy
- Food As Medicine – Monash University (online)
- Hypnosis Practitioner – American Board of Hypnotherapy
- Certified NLP Practitioner – The Association for Neuro Linguistic Programming, American Board of NLP
- Timeline Therapy Practitioner – Time Line Therapy Association
- Highly experienced in variety of meditative therapies
- Certified Sound Healer
- Certified in CPR, First Aid, Emergency life support
- Forest Healing practitioner (Shinrin-yoku)

Media Experience
- Expert guest on several major TV channel on topics including entrepreneurship, business, and mindset
- Host of sports TV-show (Dubai)

Active Experiences
- Experienced adventurer
- Avid mountain biker
- Certified in Skydiving B-license
- Certified paragliding pilot
- Motor Racing – California Superbike School, Level 2
- Tai Chi disciple

KEYNOTES, WORKSHOPS AND RETREATS

Are you a leader looking to cultivate mental wellbeing within your team, help them develop a mastery mindset, and reignite their passion?

THE SOLUTION IS KEYNOTES THAT DRIVE ACTION!

WHAT TO EXPECT WHEN YOU ENGAGE MOUSTAFA
~~Motivational speaker~~
An expert who drives change through keynotes.

The rise of digital media has opened the floodgates of noise, allowing anyone with an opinion and access to a social platform to call themselves a 'speaker'.

But if you're a decision-maker invested in your event, you want more than just an 'opinion'. Your audience deserves quality content and tangible results.

What you get:
- Research-based content
- Multidisciplinary delivery
- Lived experiences
- Engagement beyond the stage

Topics that solve business challenges

Each content theme is available as a keynote averaging 1 to 2 hours, or as a workshop and a leadership retreat ranging from half a day up to 2 full days.

Mindset Mastery
Help your team foster resilience, develop mental toughness, and use challenges for positive growth

Mindfulness and Mental Wellbeing
Master techniques that reduce workplace stress on a mental, physical, and emotional level

Passion and Purpose
Increase collaboration, talent retention, and mental wellbeing while improving work—life integration

Effective Presentation Skills
Sharpen your speaking skills and communicate in a way that gets you to YES!

For more information on booking Moustafa for your event, contact my Passion Assistant at pa@moustafa.com, visit www.moustafa.com/speaking or scan the QR code.

ONE-ON-ONE COACHING FOR VISIONARY UNDERDOGS

At any point in time, I coach a select group of passionate entrepreneurs and leaders who are driven to elevate their game.

Here to help you master your destiny!

My genuine care, tough love, and methodical approach deliver results.

Working with me liberates you from negative cycles and emotional baggage weighing you down, offers clarity on your goals and aspirations, and cultivates mindset mastery.

One thing I learned while working with some of the world's most successful people is that:

"Passionate people don't wait for life to happen to them – they happen to life."

If this sounds like you, then I'm your guy.

But ... my coaching isn't for everyone.

SLINGSHOT

There are no shortcuts to anywhere worth going, so before connecting I expect you to take 100% ownership. This means you're committed to three things:

💯 **Courage**
Being brutally honest when you face yourself in the mirror, taking 100% ownership of the results

💯 **Humility**
You ask for help when you need it, accepting the help given without being defensive or overly sensitive

💯 **Discipline**
Doing what it takes to deliver on agreements — no excuses

Together, we'll propel you toward your goals. It's not a matter of IF ... but WHEN.

Let's see if we're a good fit. Reach out to my Passion Assistant at pa@moustafa.com, visit www.moustafa.com/coaching, or scan the QR code.

BECOME A GLOBAL THOUGHT LEADER

You have spent years becoming the best in your field; now is the time to shine by becoming a bestselling author

Passionpreneur Publishing guides you through a step-by-step process to get knowledge out of your head and into a bestselling book through our unique Guided Author system.

Becoming an international author builds your legacy, gets you recognised as the 'go-to' authority in your niche and attracts more of your ideal clients.

If you are a leading Executive, Entrepreneur or professional expert and want to share your knowledge with the world get in touch with our Passion Assistant on pa@moustafa.com

You have a message to share, The world is waiting for your book.

Notes

www.ingramcontent.com/pod-product-compliance
Lightning Source LLC
Chambersburg PA
CBHW021103080526
44587CB00010B/352